P9-BIY-634

Customer Obsessed

A Whole Company Approach to Delivering Exceptional Customer Experiences

Eric Berridge

Wiley

Cover design: Bluewolf

Copyright © 2016 by Eric Berridge. All rights reserved.

Published by John Wiley & Sons, Inc., Hoboken, New Jersey.
Published simultaneously in Canada.

No part of this publication may be reproduced, stored in a retrieval system, or transmitted in any form or by any means, electronic, mechanical, photocopying, recording, scanning, or otherwise, except as permitted under Section 107 or 108 of the 1976 United States Copyright Act, without either the prior written permission of the Publisher, or authorization through payment of the appropriate per-copy fee to the Copyright Clearance Center, 222 Rosewood Drive, Danvers, MA 01923, (978) 750-8400, fax (978) 646-8600, or on the web at www.copyright.com. Requests to the Publisher for permission should be addressed to the Permissions Department, John Wiley & Sons, Inc., 111 River Street, Hoboken, NJ 07030, (201) 748-6011, fax (201) 748-6008, or online at www.wiley.com/go/permissions.

Limit of Liability/Disclaimer of Warranty: While the publisher and author have used their best efforts in preparing this book, they make no representations or warranties with the respect to the accuracy or completeness of the contents of this book and specifically disclaim any implied warranties of merchantability or fitness for a particular purpose. No warranty may be created or extended by sales representatives or written sales materials. The advice and strategies contained herein may not be suitable for your situation. You should consult with a professional where appropriate. Neither the publisher nor the author shall be liable for damages arising herefrom.

For general information about our other products and services, please contact our Customer Care Department within the United States at (800) 762-2974, outside the United States at (317) 572-3993 or fax (317) 572-4002.

Wiley publishes in a variety of print and electronic formats and by print-on-demand. Some material included with standard print versions of this book may not be included in e-books or in print-on-demand. If this book refers to media such as a CD or DVD that is not included in the version you purchased, you may download this material at http://booksupport.wiley.com. For more information about Wiley products, visit www.wiley.com.

ISBN 978-1-119-32603-8 (cloth); ISBN 978-1-119-32604-5 (ePDF);
ISBN 978-1-119-32606-9 (ePub)

Printed in the United States of America

10 9 8 7 6 5 4 3 2 1

Contents

Foreword

Fifteen years ago, Eric Berridge and I sat in a coffee shop and discussed how Salesforce would be a game changer for businesses. Salesforce had a vision to revolutionize enterprise software—with a new technology model based in the cloud, a new pay-as-you-go business model, and a new integrated corporate philanthropy model. Today, Salesforce has grown from a groundbreaking idea into a Fortune 500 company, the largest customer relationship management (CRM) company, and one of the most innovative companies in the world.

Companies of every size and industry now expect to do business with the speed, agility, and economics delivered by cloud, social, mobile, data science, and Internet of Things (IoT) technologies. Like Salesforce, Bluewolf has always prioritized the needs of customers and brought to life not just the technology but also the strategies that help customers accelerate their growth.

In his book, *Customer Obsessed: A Whole Company Approach to Delivering Exceptional Customer Experiences*, Eric shares what he has learned over the last decade and a half of helping companies create the next generation of digital experiences on the Salesforce Customer Success Platform. He looks at data, design, and culture through a customer-first lens. Utilizing data, including real-time analytics, and designing intelligent customer journeys are key to knowing customers and engaging with them across sales, service, and marketing at every touch point.

But more important than the technology is building a company culture that focuses on the well-being of all stakeholders—not just shareholders, but also employees, customers, our communities, and even the environment—to achieve the highest levels of success.

As business leaders, we have a responsibility to improve the state of the world. Contrary to what the famous economist Milton Friedman said or what many of today's business leaders think, the business of business is not just business. The business of business is to improve the state of the world, and I've found that making the world a better place and climbing the Fortune 500 rankings are not mutually exclusive.

Eric offers incisive advice for establishing a stakeholder culture and connecting at an emotional, rather than transactional, level. As he points out in the book, millennials—who make up at least 50 percent of the workforce—are teaching us that the future of work lies in creating workplaces where employees feel a higher sense of purpose. That means fully integrating values like equality, diversity, transparency, and giving back to the community into the fabric of a company.

This is what we have done at Salesforce with our equal pay initiative and our 1–1–1 integrated philanthropy model, which leverages company resources for public good by donating 1 percent of product, 1 percent of equity, and 1 percent of employee time to help nonprofits achieve their missions. Bluewolf has committed itself to diversity and giving back via the Pledge 1% movement, donating 1 percent of its equity, time, and product to nonprofits.

Foreword

This book reaffirms why Bluewolf is a leader in the cloud consulting industry and a Salesforce Global Strategic Partner. *Customer Obsessed* offers insightful, practical strategies for any CEO, entrepreneur, or business desiring to understand what it takes to be a customer-first company, establish a thriving culture, and drive success through all levels of their business.

—Marc Benioff

Preface

It's no secret that cloud computing is our global technology future, and while there are many cloud solutions available, Salesforce and its ecosystem are the dominant players in today's customer relationship management (CRM) market. They have 18.6 percent market share, their closest competitor has 6 percent, and International Data Corporation's (IDC) 2015 report highlights the tremendous growth of the Salesforce ecosystem—$272 billion in gross domestic product (GDP) impact worldwide by 2018.[1]

For over 15 years, Bluewolf has been customizing Salesforce and delivering transformative results for clients, and we're just scratching the surface of this immense opportunity. Why is that? While public cloud spending surpassed $50 billion worldwide last year, it still represents less than 3 percent of total spending on IT.[2] We are still at the inception of IT innovation, but more than ever, we're seeing companies recognize the value of Salesforce and other cloud solutions to transform their business. We are also in the midst of the evolution of design and design thinking, two business elements that are beginning to appear more and more in forward-thinking conversations. As these markets grow together, we'll start seeing some powerful results and partnerships between Salesforce and companies like IBM iX.

PREFACE

As Salesforce's longest running partner, Bluewolf has a deep understanding of how and why Salesforce's technology helps deliver an exceptional customer experience. While we consider ourselves technology agnostic, Salesforce plays a large role in our work and features prominently in many of the stories and examples you'll read in this book.

While Bluewolf uses Salesforce, the purpose of this book isn't to sell you on their particular cloud solution; it's to take you on a journey through the current digital landscape and provide insight into how to sustain competitive advantage in a diverse, rapidly evolving global economy. Whether or not you use Salesforce, this book will provide you with a strategic framework to drive business transformation for your organization and your customers, and give an understanding of how cloud technology influences, and is influenced by, current trends and developments in design, analytics, and customer and employee culture.

If your company has already embraced Salesforce, this book should help to uncover ways that you can use it to gain a better competitive advantage; if your company is thinking of using Salesforce, this book can show you how to avoid early pitfalls and become a best-in-class user of it; and, lastly, if your company uses a different solution, this book will give you the secrets to replicating the success of Salesforce in your own environment, to the extent that is possible.

Introduction

Good ideas fail all the time. At the end of every year, the technology literati draw up lists of failed inventions and enterprises, pointing out the pitfalls and mistakes made. This practice has its roots in more than schadenfreude. Their desire, and that of their readers, is to understand failure and to learn from others' stumbling blocks. They want to learn how to succeed (that is, make a profit) for themselves and their customers, and studying past failures is an excellent exercise in what *not* to do.

Great products and services are the sum of many failures, each carefully combed through to pick out the good and discard the ineffective or detrimental. Take, for example, the iPhone. When it was first released, it was—and still is—a massive success, a true game changer in mobile technology. But Apple didn't start with the iPhone; it started with the Apple Newton.

The Newton was a play for the Palm Pilot market and was released with huge fanfare—handheld, mobile, new user interface, celebrity CEO, great expectations—and yet Apple pulled the plug less than a year after its release. *Wired* magazine called it a "prophetic failure" and they were right.[1] The Newton, based on a cultural hypothetical and vision of the future, heralded a new age of technical innovation. It didn't fail because it was a terrible idea—it failed because it missed the mark in three key areas: data, design, and culture.

DATA

Data was not the Newton's strong suit. It allowed the user to input data, but it was static and didn't connect to anything—zero interaction with a larger network.

DESIGN

While the Newton looked cool, there was nothing in the design that trumped what consumers were already using. It was cheaper, faster, and easier to use a $3 notebook.

CULTURE

We weren't ready for the Newton—we didn't need it. We were barely using cell phones 22 years ago. And when a culture doesn't need something or can't see the value of it, failure is imminent.

Contrast the Newton with a product like Uber. Uber has achieved success because it delivers in ways the Newton could not—live data; simple, intuitive design; and a culture ready to embrace a ride share service that saves time and delivers a better experience.

If we were to map out Uber's success, their path to profitability would look a little something like the framework in Figure I.1.

Uber's strategy lies in delivering on those four business outcomes: acquisition, expansion, cost reduction, and retention. Not every play supports all four, but every single action involves at least one (see Figure I.2).

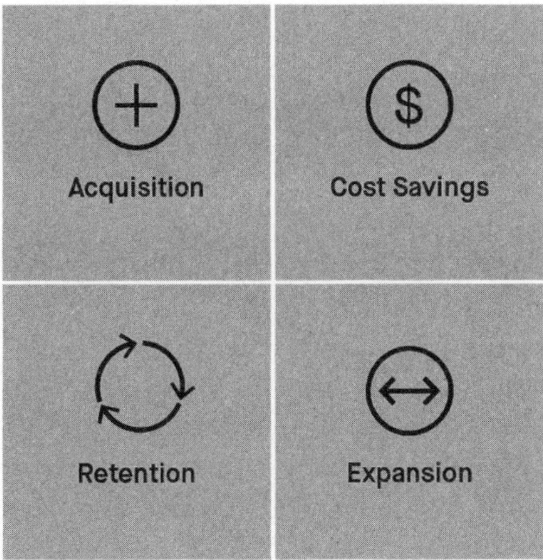

Figure I.1 Bluewolf's Business Outcomes Framework

Figure I.2 Uber Initiatives Mapped to Business Outcomes Framework

This book is about business survival for the rest of this century. It starts and ends with an obsessive focus on the customer and the ways in which customer experience is affected by other critical issues: the war for talent, employee engagement, leveraging data analytics, collaboration, creating the right culture, hiring and retaining good employees, even technology, although that last point will play the smallest part.

In today's intensely competitive digital world, there is an extremely high threshold for success, which filters out the "good enough" from the best. The purpose of this book is to provide you with a strategic framework to elevate your organization to the upper echelon of customer experience and drive profitability at all levels of your business. Here you'll find real examples of global enterprise success that Bluewolf helped guide to fruition, as well as essays by and interviews with industry leaders. Whether you have concerns about analytics, governance, or gender diversity, this book will provide the answers to the question of how to compete successfully on all fronts in the current digital landscape and deliver an exceptional customer experience.

1

Disruption and Business Success

Remember Kodak, the little yellow box factory out in Rochester, New York? They seemed like they had been part of our lives since . . . forever. But everything changes, and some organizations manage those changes better than others. When was the last time you bought a box of Kodak film, or any film for that matter?

Kodak, the photography giant, failed to navigate the shift from being a chemical company selling film and processing to the era of social media. Kodak thought it was competing with digital photography. Wrong. It clearly didn't understand its customers. Its customers were not buying digital photos. They were buying memories and creating and recreating their identities. As soon as a better alternative emerged, Kodak was toast; simply not agile enough to recognize and make the change.

So, what was that better alternative for creating identities? Facebook started it all, followed by other social media giants like Instagram and Twitter. And you can count on the memory-making business changing again. Maybe it will come in the form of the Apple watch or another type of wearable, or maybe in the form of something altogether different.

But just imagine if Kodak had built a bridge from film to digital photography to digital identity and then conceived social networking. It might be singing a completely different song today, a much happier one.

Growing up, I remember watching sweet, sappy Kodak TV ads around the holidays. They were filled with creating and sharing images of families and friends, loved ones, aging parents and grandparents, babies, new boyfriends and girlfriends. It was about capturing and replaying the customer's memories and using them to build their identities. Kodak approached the social revolution threshold, but never took those last few steps.

Not only do companies like Kodak change, but customers change, too. Today's customers are like water—they will seek the lowest point, driven by gravity to save time, to lessen the friction of buying, to align with products and services that provide transparency and objectivity and help them preserve memories and form and reform their identities again and again.

That's how I started this book—by focusing on customer identities and customer service. Customer focus is *not* about the heroic moments—it's not The Ritz-Carlton finding and returning the stuffed animal left behind by a guest's child. Yes, the Ritz excels at customer service, but that has little to do with finding lost stuffed animals. Great customer service is really about knowing what a guest needs even before the guest knows; it's realizing the photos are not just about memories, but also about identity. It's about noticing that a guest will be delayed due to weather or a flight disruption and won't arrive until 2 AM. Knowing that, you send the room key code to the customer's mobile device so they can go straight to their room upon arrival without even stopping at the check-in desk.

Better yet, heroic customer service is Berkshire Hathaway Travel rebooking your connecting flight because they know you're still sitting on the tarmac. They immediately text you updated travel details, relieving you of the worry and aggravation of further delays. Or it's your cloud software vendor serving you tangible data about your usage, which actually helps you to drive more return out of your investment.

Customer service and customer engagement used to rely on the heroic moment—the rare action that becomes a legendary tale of customer engagement which was heroic mainly because it was rare and unexpected. In that dark, murky, vendor-driven world of the past 50 years, customers often had little choice but to simply take what came. When exceptional service truly happened, it occurred because someone went out of the way to actually recognize a customer need and align with it without being asked.

Today, customer engagement has shifted. Customers don't just take what they get; they arrive with an expectation that the brand—the vendor—knows what the customer wants before they do. Paul Papas, head of IBM iX, put it perfectly when he said, "The last best experience anyone has anywhere becomes the minimum expectation for the experience they want everywhere." Companies need to master customer engagement in order to *become* that last best experience. Customer engagement is defined by making every customer moment count, regardless of who is delivering it. And to make every moment count, we have to know who our customers are, where they are, what they are experiencing, and what they like and need. On top of all of that, we then have to act on that information and be correct most of the time.

This isn't as hard as it might seem. One of the biggest changes we have seen in the past five years is a customer's willingness to reveal personal information in an effort to receive better service. In 2011, I gave a presentation to a group of about 100 students at MIT. I asked them point blank: raise your hand if it disturbs you that Facebook is selling your data. Not a single hand went up. Now couple this willingness to share personal information with the availability of social tools to broadcast these likes and dislikes, and suddenly the vendor of yesteryear is presented with a new challenge and an astonishing opportunity to serve the individual tastes and desires of all of its customers. Yet, most still don't get it, and that's the reason for this book.

The challenge comes from the fact that the consumer and the customer are moving faster than legacy vendors can react. That's why start-ups often succeed against established brands. Start-ups have the ability to quickly leverage the network effect of our connected world to leapfrog basic services and expose almost every established business to one threat or another. That's always been the case, of course, only now it seems to be happening faster and more often.

So what do customers actually want? There are many answers, as many as the 7.4 billion people on the planet, but after a six-year global polling effort encompassing 150 countries, Jim Clifton, Chairman and CEO of Gallup and author of *The Coming Jobs War*, was able to reduce it to one: what the world wants is a good job.[1] This seems ridiculously trivial until you parse the sentence. The key word is *good*.

To succeed at customer obsession and engagement, companies need to find, hire, and retain people who will be engaged in the organization and, most important, with the customer regardless of whether the customer or the interaction falls specifically under their job description. Engaged, customer-focused employees at all levels are required if a company is to become customer obsessed and experience the success that invariably follows.

Clifton wasn't referring to jobs bagging groceries in a supermarket or ripping admission tickets at the neighborhood cinema complex (another industry desperately remaking itself in the face of streaming media options that dramatically change how customers view movies; essentially anywhere, at any time, from any device, at a range of prices). He was referring to the kind of jobs you need to offer to build an effective customer-obsessed organization. To Clifton, a good job means a job that gives the worker sufficient, steady work that will sustain them over time. He goes on to write: "A good job defines your relationship with your city, your country, and the whole world around you."[2] That also includes the vendors of products and services whose customers will be spending some of the proceeds of that good job with them. Those are the people a customer-obsessed organization needs if it is to know and anticipate what its customers and prospective customers need, even before they know it.

True customer engagement and customer obsession happens when a brand is aligned with a need, and until now, too many brands have survived focused on their own needs, not the customers' needs. Does the legacy brand attitude in Figure 1.1 sound familiar?

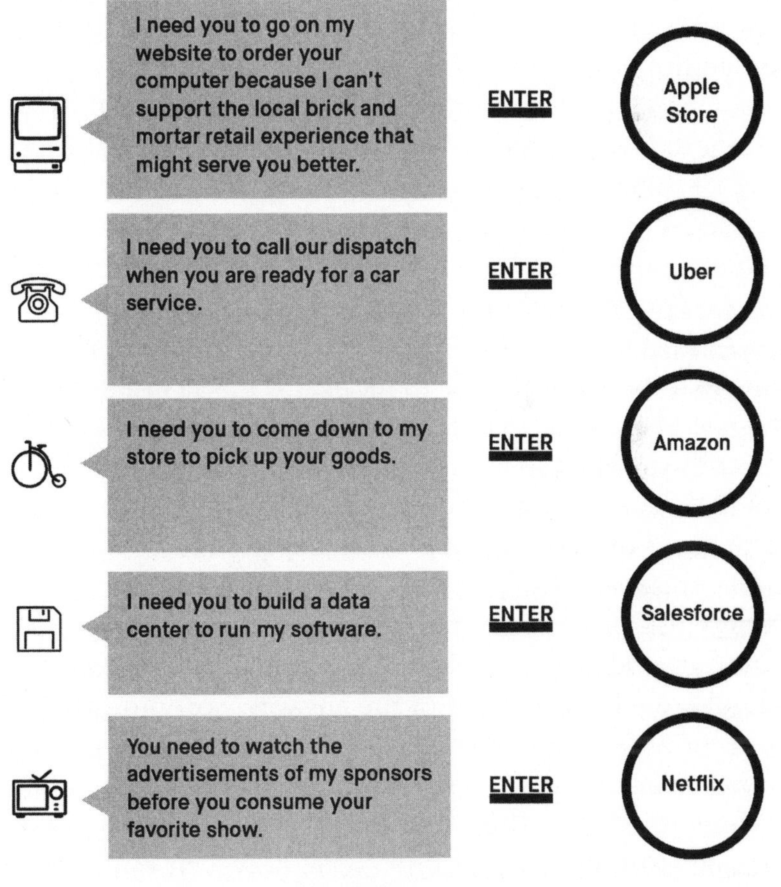

FIGURE 1.1

Businesses across the world are being disrupted and upended because the rise of digital has enabled some organizations to identify the true needs and desires of customers and fulfill them. And alignment with those needs requires organizations to completely rethink their go-to-market approach and, perhaps even most important, to rethink their employee culture, which lives at the heart of customer engagement.

Maybe your business is one of those being disrupted and upended, or you suspect it is vulnerable to that. Congratulations; reading this book is a good first move. Or maybe you are one of the disrupters who fear you could also be upended someday. This book will help you, too, by showing what you need to keep the momentum going.

Let's start with the assumption that your business already has customers or you expect to have some. Let's also assume that you have, or intend to have, employees and partners (suppliers, providers—whatever you want to call them). I present these assumptions because the days of the lone wolf are over. No business (and certainly no individual) can do it all alone. Collaboration is the new byword for success. That means you are going to have to collaborate to succeed. The era of the vertically integrated enterprise that did everything it needed to create and deliver the product to the customer ended in the first half of the twentieth century. Like it or not, it is a new era. The landscape has changed dramatically and continues to shift. Think Netflix. Think Amazon. Think Apple.

Our world is fast becoming customer-centric. Just listen to the chatter around big data. That might lead you to believe that technology will provide all of the answers. Sorry to disappoint, but technology alone cannot save you in this new customer-centric, collaborative world. This really is not about technology. Is it important? Yes. But no technology gadget will be a savior. The power of the network and social, however, can be a game changer when done right. The instinct of the upstarts to leverage the power of social networks is one reason they are able to leapfrog established enterprise players. Technology that can make frictionless, unnoticed connections with the customer is valuable. But even then, technology alone isn't enough.

To remain relevant, companies must continuously innovate to deliver an exceptional customer experience. The way to do that is to not only be customer-centric but customer-obsessed. To do this, company leaders must be focused on driving customer obsession throughout the entire company. That means you need to enable your employees to understand your customers as people with individual stories. You also need to tie that focus to the delivery of specific, measurable outcomes. Customer focus without an understanding of how it impacts your bottom line may help in the beginning, but it won't be enough to drive and maintain profitable, positive change.

Think about it: customers don't care about being served by the so-called right department. Instead, empower your employees to own any customer interaction they touch—however and whenever it may occur. Customers don't care if they are working with someone in accounting, production, or sales. They want their needs met and even anticipated, whenever and wherever you can do it. This kind of customer-centric service requires the free flow of information and collaborative knowledge, which means tight integration between back-end accounting and enterprise resource planning (ERP) systems, front-end customer relationship management (CRM) systems, and anything else that can help satisfy the customer's need. Internal silos must become invisible or nonexistent. Information should flow freely among departments and employees, between everyone and anyone who might encounter the customer in the effort to solve their problems or questions.

Granted, such innovation and engagement across the enterprise has the potential to be chaotic. Companies must be willing to embrace some chaos for the sake of succeeding in the emerging customer engagement economy, which dictates companies continuously respond to—and preferably get ahead of—the needs of their customers. To that end, every employee and customer touch point must be mobilized to better understand customer needs and improve customer engagement. At the beginning of this chapter, I referenced Berkshire Hathaway's response to travel difficulties. Their story offers a compelling example of how to understand and engage with customers.

Berkshire Hathaway Story

BACKGROUND

Berkshire Hathaway Travel Protection (BHTP) is a division of Berkshire Hathaway Specialty Insurance, which provides commercial property, casualty, healthcare liability, and professional insurance for customers across the United States. BHTP has reinvented travel insurance for today's mobile consumer and the evolving airline industry with AirCare™, travel insurance designed specifically for airline flights that proactively monitors and pays claims when travel mishaps arise.

THE PROBLEM

While the insurance industry handles highly personal information, it has been slow to adopt personalized, customer-focused technology solutions. BHTP wanted to design a new, disruptive consumer travel-insurance product, but needed partners to build out a system that leveraged flight data, processed claims, and provided the customer-engagement platform. What BHTP was looking for was a one-stop-shop travel-insurance app that would facilitate communication between the service agent and the customer across all channels. To accomplish this BHTP engaged Bluewolf to help build the platform needed to launch AirCare.

THE SOLUTION

Bluewolf helped BHTP develop the back-end systems to build out their one-of-a-kind AirCare insurance. The result was an end-to-end policy administration system on the Salesforce1 platform. We integrated BHTP's policy data into Salesforce, which was then integrated with a quoting tool for generating policy quotes, Drawloop for document creation and automation, Amazon S3 for document storage, and a payment processor that connected to BHTP's backend general ledger. The app became a real-time system of record, allowing information to flow continuously from policy conception through claim administration.

Bluewolf focused on building an insurance app that also acted as a cloud-based personal concierge service, with SMS and social media integrated into more traditional channels, like e-mail and phone. This allows BHTP to provide travelers with mobile updates and communications through various social channels. The integration paired AirCare with Salesforce Marketing Cloud as well as the Salesforce Service Console, and implemented a robust agent interface that allowed agents to interact with customers through their channel of choice.

THE RESULTS

Bluewolf helped BHTP build and launch AirCare in just six weeks. BHTP assists AirCare customers with travel itinerary repairs, helps locate lost luggage quickly, monitors flight status in real-time, and can even help travelers get access to airport club lounges—all via text, e-mail, web chat, and even Twitter. The platform serves a new generation of travelers and gives them simpler, smarter coverage that can be managed end-to-end on a mobile device. Its proactive claim processing pays claims in seconds using a myriad of electronic payment platforms, with funds transferred directly to the traveler's bank account.

(*continued*)

(continued)

By providing the right information at the right time, BHTP can manage and report on the entire customer journey. Today, BHTP uses this system to process all its claims across multiple product lines, giving the company the power to personalize the customer experience and develop new ways to service travelers.

I consider this kind of customer obsession and engagement the essential organizing principle of twenty-first-century enterprise success. It is the only viable response to the emergence of a customer-centric world that calls for implementing strategies that fall somewhere between a wrecking ball that demolishes all you have been doing and lip service where you say the right things but make no changes that reflect what you just said. Although the wrecking ball produces heroic customer-focused actions here and there, it is not enough. A better strategy is to embark on a steady process to change the corporate mind-set by incorporating a modest customer focus in almost everything you do, at every stage of customer interaction. Over time, this approach can embed a customer focus throughout the organization gradually and nondisruptively. Surprisingly, it is these subtle changes that become the real game changers as they are replicated throughout the DNA of the organization. Approached in this way, becoming customer focused and even customer obsessed is not difficult. Any organization could do it. Notice I said they *could* do it. Most won't. Again, since you're reading this book, you actually might.

So, what are the real and lasting game changers? Here's a short list that will come up in more detail in subsequent chapters:

- Social media—how well you know your customers and how fast you act on that insight can be a big game changer, and keeping that information updated in real time is essential. That means keep updating what you know every hour of every day.

- Collaboration among staff, partners and associates, and customers is now essential; the closer and deeper the collaboration the better.
- Culture takes on increasingly greater importance; you have to cultivate a customer-obsessed environment involving everyone, all the time.
- Finding, nurturing, motivating, and keeping good talent is key to winning. Look for people with an aptitude for customer service.
- Data is everything when it comes to engaging and satisfying customers. It's the best way to learn about the customer and keep learning throughout the (hopefully very long) relationship.
- Insightful, integrated data analytics in absolute real time; without real-time analytics, data quickly becomes worthless.

Ultimately, you want to establish a strategic framework and foundation that is obsessed with the customer and can withstand the pressures of a business world constantly in flux. This isn't easy. It requires you to shift your focus from the intangible goals that sound so good in sound bites, to measuring your success against business outcomes. You have to speak differently with the customer, hire different people and manage them differently, work with providers and partners in new ways, leverage your resources, and evaluate and deploy technology unlike how you have before. That's what this book will show you. Get ready for an exciting ride.

2

People Drive Change, Technology Enables

I am a firm believer that people, not technology, are the driving force behind a company's success. Don't believe me? Let's take a look at one of the most people-focused organizations operating today: Change.org. Their entire purpose is to enable collective action to drive positive change; people connecting with other people, aided by technology. Completely user driven, their online petition platform enables people all over the world to create campaigns to accomplish incredible things: overturning the ban on gay Boy Scouts, defeating Thailand's blanket amnesty bill, saving Meriam Yehya Ibrahim Ishag in Sudan from execution on apostasy charges, and the list goes on. Over 100 million people have used Change.org since it launched in 2007, and it isn't because of the technology supporting it.[1] The company tapped into an incredibly powerful force to help make a difference in the world: people.

Now, I know that not every company can operate like Change.org, but there are a ton of other examples where companies put people, and their experiences first. Take a look at companies like

USAA and Trader Joe's, two radically different businesses, but with the same goal in mind: serving the customer. While they use technology to improve the customer experience, they never allow new technology to dictate or alter that focus. That's what I mean when I say companies need to prioritize people over technology. Every company's success is dependent upon people, whether they're customers, partners, or employees. Getting in that mindset is essential to providing a better experience across every aspect of your business.

TECHNOLOGY GAME CHANGERS

Not every advance in technology, no matter how innovative, is a game changer. Similarly, technology itself is often not the answer. Sometimes even the seemingly best technology doesn't deliver. Remember Google Glass, the wearable computer and video recorder? The early adopters who shelled out big bucks were the stars of the party among the digital cognoscenti. However, the press attention eventually died down, and today Google Glass is an anachronism before its time. Google's product development team is already working on a new and improved form, but it wasn't a game changer then and it may never be.

Maybe the exception that proves the rule is the Apple Watch. It continues to attract customers despite its large price tag and limited functionality. The Apple Watch helped propel iOS 8 adoption to 81 percent by the end of April 2015.[2] Still, popularity does not necessarily mean a technology is a game changer. Neither does a mob of imitators at different price points. The Apple Watch, and wearables as a general category, may eventually produce a revolutionary product or two, but that's far from a given.

It takes more than just cool technology and a flood of adoring press coverage to produce a product that becomes pervasive. Technology adoption is driven by unique moments where users experience a huge upgrade. Picture the first time you used an iPod versus a CD player or Uber instead of a yellow cab—these moments blended simplicity with a massive improvement in experience.

So how do we identify true habit-forming products or, more important, build them ourselves? Either business culture is advancing faster than technical innovation or innovation is advancing faster than the business. Neither situation is conducive to game changers, and cool alone is not enough. The world is full of problem solvers, but few problem finders. Do the research and discover the problems for which people lack a simple solution and build it. Take social media. People have always loved talking about themselves and sharing memories. Social media gave them an easy way to do it. Again, Kodak was so close, but never quite got social media. To a certain extent, social media allows you to continually reinvent yourself with each social interaction as Kodak customers did with the photos they took, showed, and saved. But better than paper-based photos, social media brings with it a dynamic network with a built-in audience: friends and followers and friends of friends and followers. What's not to like?

Nir Eyal addresses the quandary of creating addictive products that become pervasive in his book *Hooked: How to Build Habit-Forming Products* (Portfolio, 2014). Habit-forming products are not necessarily synonymous with game-changing technology. Still, if we want addictive products that we can't put down, how do we create them and do so consistently? Simple: you manufacture them following Eyal's formula.

As Eyal explains in the book: "Today, small startup teams can profoundly change behavior by guiding users through a series of experiences I call hooks. The more often users run through these hooks, the more likely they are to form habits."[3] When joined to a compelling innovation, these usage habits result in a long-lived hit product. Companies do this through what Eyal calls the hook model, a four-phase process (see Figure 2.1) to stimulate

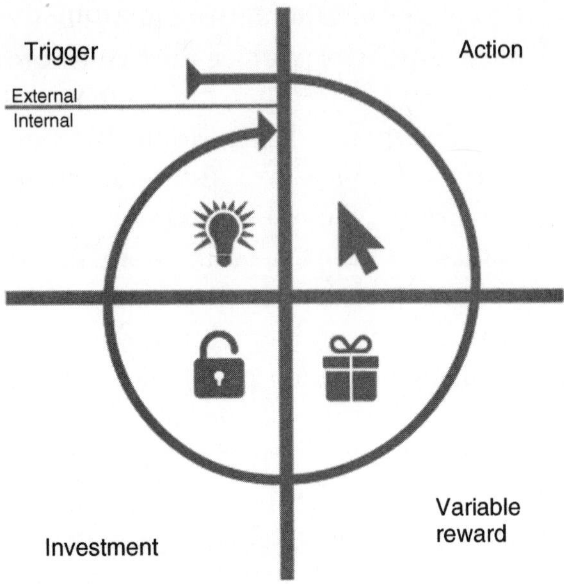

Figure 2.1 Eyal's Hook Canvas Identifies Four Phases in a Loop

propensity of customers to form habits around the product. "Through consecutive hook cycles, successful products reach their ultimate goal of unprompted user engagement, bringing users back repeatedly, without depending on costly advertising or aggressive messaging," Eyal writes.[4] To stimulate the hook cycle, Eyal created the hook model or hook canvas, which consists of four steps or phases: trigger, action, variable reward, and investment. The investment is something the user makes, which can be configuring and personalizing the product or even just learning to use it. For example, no matter how useful a watch is, it remains functionally worthless if the user hasn't made the investment in learning how to tell time.

From the perspective of business outcomes, the trigger is the most important aspect of the product. Answering the question of why you want the customer to use your product—that is, how it drives profitability—and why the customer will want to use the product will help define and refine your customer focus and keep you accountable to delivering on your metrics for success.

BUILD PEOPLE RELATIONSHIPS, NOT TECHNOLOGY PRODUCTS

I am not opposed to technology. To the contrary, I built my business on helping people use new technology effectively and efficiently. However, it is more important to build relationships with people, especially the workers and partners and, most important, customers and prospective customers. Pound for pound, these relationships will deliver greater value than the latest iPhone or Uber or whatever hot new technology that comes along. Apple doesn't succeed on the basis of cool technology alone. Apple delivers value by designing its products through the eyes of its customers and establishing a great connection through empathy and superior service. If your aim is to succeed as a customer-obsessed business, building dynamic relationships with people is vital. Once you have secured the relationship, you're better equipped to build an irresistible customer experience through the empathy you have gained.

Still, some technology can help you build these human relationships in key ways:

- Expedite two-way or even X-way interactive communications through teleconferencing capabilities.
- Enhance personal relationships through more frequent, timely, and deeper real-time communications.
- Tap human emotion and intellect through omnichannel experiences and virtual reality.

For the purposes of this book, I recommend using technology to advance and enrich the personal business relationship. Along the same lines, it should support and further your goals within the existing structure and environment.

RULES FOR ENGAGED, CUSTOMER-FOCUSED BUSINESSES

There are a handful of rules that can ensure you achieve and sustain a truly customer-obsessed organization. The first is to listen to the customer. Sounds pretty self-evident, right? But you'd be amazed at how many companies fail to do so.

What I mean is to *truly* listen to the customer. To do that, don't listen to the customer with an agenda in your mind or for the opportunity to interject one or two of your own ideas or make a sale. Instead, you have to listen to what the customer is actually saying right then, at that moment; what it means, what it might mean, and what it clearly doesn't mean. That requires you to take off your consultant-sales hat or your service-manager hat, or any other hats you might wear. Then, listen with your customer hat, which is simply that—listening to the customer. It doesn't involve objecting, selling, educating, or analyzing. It means listening to the customer and taking the appropriate action based on what the customer has said or maybe not said. If you actually listen, you'll figure it out.

Here are some other rules that will assist in establishing a customer-obsessed organization:

- No one owns the customer but someone always owns the moment. Seize each of those moments before somebody else does. Everyone in the enterprise should act like they own the customer and feel empowered to seize each moment expressly for the purpose of delivering outstanding customer service.

- Find your equilibrium. This really is about you and your organization. You need to define what your enterprise is and what it means to every customer. Unfortunately, for some customers, your organization may not mean much to them at all; it may be just another replaceable cog. (That may be the most important thing you hear—if you are astute enough to catch it, probe for more insight, and then act on it.)
- Identify and establish the natural rhythm of your organization—every organization has one. When people are puzzled by this statement, I point to the Salesforce product release cycle as an example of an organization's natural rhythm. Once you have identified your organization's natural rhythm, try to sync it with that of your customers, partners, staff, and other key stakeholders.
- Keep your bearings in a fluid landscape. Since the advent of the cloud and cloud computing, the business landscape has been as fluid as it gets. Things continually change. The only sensible response is to avoid setting your business process, architecture, policies, and procedures in concrete. Design your business for maximum flexibility, but also maintain consistency.
- Engage your people to the max. They want to be engaged and contribute in ways you may not even realize. Your staff produces the multiplier effect, the added profitable production that comes from the efforts of your staff, a gain MBA professors like to harp on. The more you can engage your staff, the more you can stimulate the multiplier effect.
- Tap into human emotion. Done in the right way, at the right time, it is the most powerful tool you have. Automation is great, but it has known limits and constraints.

- Be constantly alert to new, existing, and vampire competition. These are unnoticed competitors that ghost around in the background and shadows until they suddenly emerge into the light and quickly become a force to be reckoned with. These can often be the most dangerous, especially vampire competitors (those previously dead). They can and do arise; just look at Nokia and BlackBerry.
- Continually explore the role of technology. First, notice how technology is last on this list. It's not the most important thing, but you still need to constantly monitor technology advances and keep an eye on those that may advance your business goals or open new opportunities you haven't considered. It will be interesting to see, as of this writing, what new nascent opportunities arise from the Internet of Things, cognitive computing, and virtual reality.

Despite the simplicity of the steps listed previously, becoming a customer-obsessed organization isn't as easy as it may seem. Most organizations and people automatically assume they know what change is called for and what technology is required to implement such a change. Often, they are flat out wrong, and there is a lot of risk for the organization involved. Plans can be set back or completely derailed. Expenses are incurred and may not be easily absorbed or written off. The reality is that the technology endgame must be constantly investigated, experiments engaged, failures encountered, and investigated again.

My contention is not that technology can't do the job. Rather, it's that even the best technology is not necessarily good enough or sufficient. Adoption is never assured. Technological change in today's world needs to be embraced by individuals who have short attention spans and will not read a manual. Intuitive design is the key to capturing these people, and intuitive design is still more the exception than the norm.

That leaves us with collaborative communal enterprises obsessed with creating the best customer experiences. And it all starts with being a good listener.

HOW TO BE A GOOD LISTENER

To be a good listener you have to be interested in what the other person has to say. Seems incredibly self-evident, but how many people do you speak with who aren't really interested in what you have to say? More to the point, how many people do you speak with that *you* aren't really interested in what they have to say, either? Or maybe, you're interested only until you get some piece of information that you need for some other purpose. After that your interest in the coversation takes a nosedive.

To be a really good listener, you have to be sincerely interested in what the other person is actually saying. When Joel Peterson, chairman of JetBlue Airways, was interviewed by *The New York Times* about the reasons for his success as an executive, this particular answer stood out:

> A lot of it is listening. I'm a really good listener. It's not a technique—I'm really interested in what people have to say. But it does develop trust as a byproduct. If you're authentic, open, you call things as they are, you really are direct and you listen well, that develops trust.

He also talked about not bringing your agenda if you want to do a good job at listening:

> And you can't have an agenda. When you have your own agenda when you're listening to someone, what you're doing is you're formulating your response rather than

(*continued*)

> *(continued)*
> processing what the other person is saying. You have to really be at home with yourself. If you have these driving needs to show off or be heard or whatever, then that kind of overwhelms the process. If you're really grounded and at home with yourself, then you can actually get in the other person's world, and I think that builds trust too.[5]

People are often listening closely, but they still have their agenda. They are listening for clues that will enable them to advance their agenda, maybe later in the conversation, maybe in a follow-up conversation. If the other party is a customer, you really want to connect with them, but more often than not, you sacrifice the value of being customer focused for another agenda item.

So, short of having the patience or forbearance of a saint, how does Peterson really listen closely? Here's what he actually does:

> I ask a lot of "why" questions. I'll ask people to tell me their story, and then you're listening for inflection points. Everybody changes course, and the great question then is why and why again and then why again. Once you start to understand why people have done things you can fully understand their story.

Customer obsession is about getting as deeply as you can into the customer's own narrative with all of its many twists and turns.

Let's boil these ideas down to a handful of key points:

- Listen attentively to build trust.
- Demonstrate interest by asking questions and more questions.
- Be direct, authentic, open, and honest.

- Don't bring an agenda; leave all of your other hats somewhere else.
- Resist the urge to formulate an immediate response unless it's to ask another question.
- Bring zen to bear—get really grounded; feel at home with yourself before entering a customer's world.
- Ask why repeatedly. Then ask why and why again.

Good listening lies at the heart of the communal enterprise and customer obsession.

COMMUNAL ENTERPRISE—RISE OF REED'S LAW

Customer obsession works best as a communal and collaborative undertaking. This is due to the power of Reed's law, first proposed by David P. Reed, a computer science professor at MIT. Reed's law is similar to Moore's law, but focuses on network expansion rather than processor density. Reed's law suggests that the power of the network, particularly a social network, increases exponentially with the size of the network (see Figure 2.2). (Similarly, Moore's law postulated that computing capacity would double every 18–24 months, which led to decades of continuous drops in computer processor costs. It worked until a few years ago, when the physics of miniaturization caught up to it.)

So why should those who are interested in communal enterprises and social networks care about Reed's law? Because even if the utility of groups available to be joined is very small on a peer-group basis, eventually the network effect of potential group membership can dominate the overall economics of the system since any individual can connect separately with any other

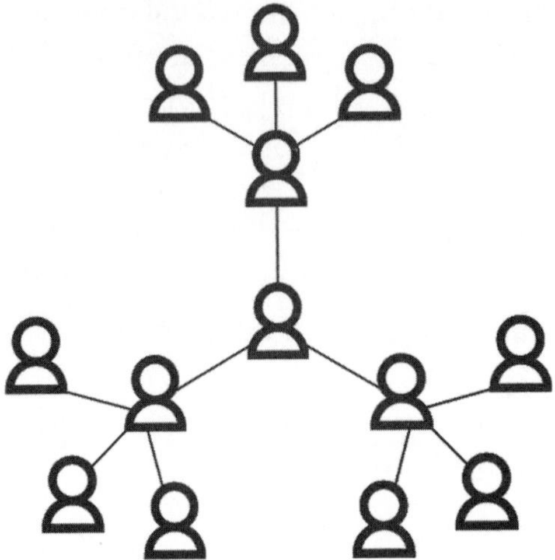

Figure 2.2 Reed's Law of Social Network Expansion

member. And it is the overall economics of the system that you care about.

Reed's law theoretically could lead to a wiki-culture with billions of people engaged in untold collaborations. This is also how the astounding projections of the growth of the Internet of Things quickly reach into the trillions by the next decade. The communal enterprise presents the best engine of sustained innovation, customer service, and social collaboration.

Some final thoughts on the human communal enterprise that drives change: it is a social, collaborative world, and until you experience social and see it in action, it is hard to understand. It is not something you can appreciate in the abstract.

In the same way, you can't appreciate the power of collaboration until you have collaborated and experienced its value. Participation requires more than offering moral support or approving a budget. Participation requires digging in, mixing it up, and maybe getting a little dirty. Finally, the communal enterprise is not some totalitarian order. The individuals involved—and they are all individuals—need freedom and empowerment. They need to be encouraged to experiment, take risks, and initiate actions. Otherwise, the communal enterprise becomes stagnant and cannot drive any change at all, and certainly cannot take initiative on behalf of the customer.

3

Why Social Matters to Every Business

In Google's 2011 study analyzing the evolution of the mobile consumer, Australia suddenly went from a low smartphone adoption locale the year before (2010) to one of the world's leaders in smartphone adoption in 2011.[1] That's a pretty big change in a relatively short period of time.

Maybe not so coincidentally, Australia also experienced a big uptick in social media usage, which altered the communication mix. People changed their communication patterns, habits, and spending seemingly overnight. Vodafone, a leading carrier in Australia, was caught flat-footed and faced well-publicized criticism relating to service and network issues, especially the time it took to respond to this customer-instigated change.

And how did those customers vent their feelings? Via social media, not surprisingly. They quickly took to social channels—Facebook, Twitter, blogs, and communities—to voice their concerns. According to Erik Jacobsen, online development and system strategy manager at Vodafone at the time, the company saw a whopping 2,500 percent growth in social media!

Remember, all this occurred over a short time period, from one year to the next, and was not something that had been percolating below the surface for years. What people were saying was something Vodafone sorely needed to hear: the company's service delivery had fallen well below customer expectations.

"We knew that listening to our customers and responding quickly was the only way to address these negative perceptions on social channels. We had to close the gap between customer service expectations and delivery," Jacobsen said. And they had to do it fast: there was no time to form a planning committee to craft a three- or five-year social media vision and strategy and execute it.

Instead, Vodafone turned to one of the leading social networking providers, Salesforce, and quickly adopted their Service Cloud platform, which allowed flexibility in customization and collaboration across service channels. Then Vodafone formed a knowledge management team to assemble the more relevant information customers were requesting most often, information that could be easily tagged, shared, and posted across a variety of social channels. But even that wasn't enough. To capture the resulting social intelligence, Vodafone integrated the Radian6™ Console, a social media monitoring and engagement platform, and also implemented Social Hub, which pushes Twitter, Facebook, and blog posts through Service Cloud as real-time cases.

It worked! Within six months of moving to the Service Cloud and adopting a suite of social tools, Vodafone had quadrupled the number of social interactions with its customers. Since 2011, organic visits to the site have doubled and content quality ratings have shot up 800 percent. Vodafone is now leading the industry in social media response in Australia and has delivered a dramatically improved customer experience.

At the end of 2013, Vodafone decided to shift from big ticket branding—sponsorships and the like—to increased one-to-one personalization via social media.[2] They continue to refine and expand their social media strategy to go beyond connecting with customers to resolve issues. Today, Vodafone's social campaigns focus on storytelling, drawing in current and potential users with engaging photos and posts designed to evoke an experience, memory, or desire. Take a moment to look at Vodafone's Twitter feed. You'll see a combination of direct customer interaction, pertinent news, and their unique brand of storytelling. It's no longer about big, flashy ad campaigns—it's about improving the customer experience through personal relationships, enabled by social.

Their customers spoke and Vodafone listened. The key was adopting tech to support the social initiative that transformed their business rather than ignoring the message it was delivering. This wasn't rocket science; anybody could do it. The technology—smartphones, social media, data analytics—had already been around for a few years. Vodafone could have gotten the message on its own earlier, but it took hearing it from unhappy people to drive the change.

The lesson I take from the Vodafone experience and pass along to our people at Bluewolf is to take what you hear from customers and prospects on social media very seriously. These aren't fringe voices; they're your future.

WHY SOCIAL?

Social isn't just for kids or teenagers, or even millennials. Baby boomers use it heavily, as do the elderly (often to communicate with grandchildren). In short, everyone who has access to the Internet can use social. And most everybody does. Statistica projects 2.44 billion social media users worldwide by 2018.[3] That is about one-third of the population of the planet.

As important, people take social seriously. According to the Pew Research organization, roughly two-thirds (64 percent) of U.S. adults use Facebook, and half of those get their news

Figure 3.1 1/3 Global Population Gets their News from Facebook

there—amounting to 30 percent of the general population (Figure 3.1).[4] That's better reach than most TV news operations, even the big network nightly news broadcasts.

The social online phenomenon's popularity is ironic because it connects back to our most basic, atavistic human urges: the desire to connect with others as part of a community and the need to communicate. In that sense, you don't get much more basic than social media.

In his classic work, *Walden*, Henry David Thoreau championed the individual and the solitary life. What many people don't realize is how often Thoreau hosted visitors. He also walked the mile-and-a-half to see his mother regularly and called on friends during his 22-month experiment at Walden Pond. (To this day you can walk the same path that Thoreau took from his cottage to Ralph Waldo Emerson's House [see Figure 3.2].) The champion of asceticism and self-sufficiency couldn't escape this very human fact: we thrive best in a social society; we need human contact. And that is what social media brings us and why as business managers this is a gift we don't want to spurn. To the contrary, we want to take maximum advantage of social, and this chapter will show you how to do it.

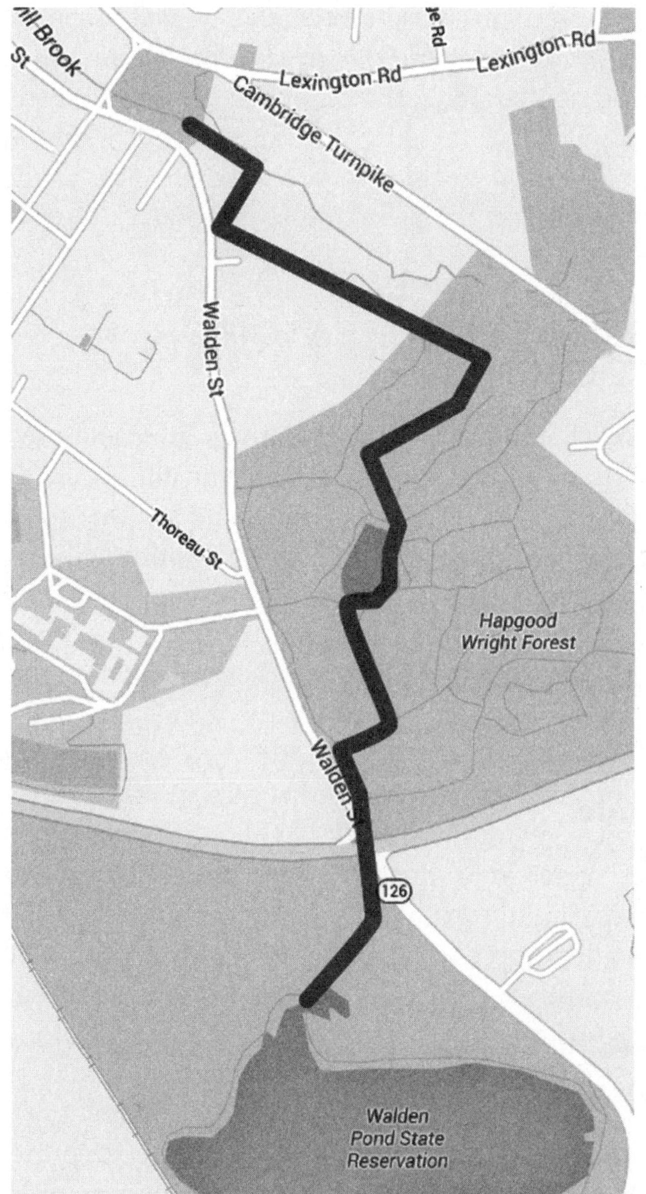

Figure 3.2 Emerson-Thoreau Amble at Walden Pond

The key human characteristics that social enhances are the need to communicate and the drive to understand one another. In the case of Vodafone, the company was shocked to realize it had clearly failed at meeting the expectations of customers and prospects. When it mended its ways and was able to meet those expectations, good things started to happen.

"SOCIAL MEDIA: CREATOR OR DESTROYER?"

On February 3, 2016, Thomas Friedman wrote an op-ed entitled "Social Media: Destroyer or Creator?" In the article, Friedman extensively quotes Wael Ghonim, one of the social media architects behind the 2012 Egyptian revolution. Ghonim asserts that social media is filled with too many destroyers, those people who cannot or will not engage in civil discussion on message boards and comment sections, and that sustained revolutions (or even more moderate movements for change) are not currently possible. Ghonim thinks that current use of social media creates self-serving echo chambers and that that was the primary reason the Egyptian revolution didn't have long-lasting success.[5]

I both agree and disagree with the assertion that social encourages one-directional communication. It depends on the medium and its user community. Let's take a look at one of the most successful social and political movements in recent history, civil rights. This movement was years in the making, it was highly organized, and had identifiable leaders. And it wasn't just Dr. King; it was an entire dedicated, mobilized organization. Rosa Parks was one of three women considered to protest by not giving up her seat on the bus. The movement's leadership vetted all of them completely, deciding that Parks had the cleanest, most unobjectionable background, so that her strong, simple action couldn't be detracted from by skeletons in her past. These organizers were methodical, pragmatic, unrelenting, and bold. So yes, social media is a great facilitator of communication and comes with its own unique set of challenges, but successful movements can't be faceless. The Egyptian revolution's problem wasn't only that social media helped spread as much misinformation as truth, but that there was no centrality, no coalition, no leaders to whom those social media masses could look for guidance.

Looking at social media and the Internet as the ultimate solution (or problem) to the challenges facing revolution and true change is myopic. Internet discussion boards aren't only filled with angry trolls—there are already a number of sites that exist today that encourage deeper, more thoughtful debate and conversation. I appreciate the fact that Ghonim and his team are creating more opportunities for that, but to say that it doesn't already exist is misleading. There will always be detractors, misinformation, and outright lies that face these types of movements. This has been true since time immemorial, from graffiti, to public speeches, to pamphleteering and newspapers, to radio and television. We've simply expanded that field via the Internet, and while it's easier than ever to respond to antagonists or be one yourself, it's also easier to begin and sustain positive movements for change, provided that true organization and leadership is in place. There will still be push and pull over who should "be the leaders," but without them to rally around, those movements are often doomed to failure (or the sometimes equally horrifying success of the masses and mob mentality, e.g. the French Revolution. Positive, perhaps, in the end result, but a terrifying and bloody era all the same.)

The same can be said for social media initiatives at the company level (albeit on a much smaller scale). Without broad guidance, clear goals, and community leaders, social media promotion and engagement, both internally and externally, won't be successful.

SOCIAL CAN CHANGE EVERYTHING

It certainly did here at Bluewolf. Seven years ago when I published *Iterate or Die*, social was barely on our radar screen. In the last few years, it has emerged as one of the mainstays of Bluewolf, a central part of our culture, and a key contributor to our growth and success.

We have made a huge investment in social and its gamification component via a customized program we call Prime, Bluewolf's internal engagement program designed to motivate and reward employees for participating in social activities that help enhance our brand at all levels, both internally and externally. In fact, last year we sent the top 50 gamification scorers, each with a personal guest, to Hawaii for a weeklong, all-expense-paid vacation. This trip, the culmination of our gamification initiative, generated huge enthusiasm among our global staff over the course of the year. In the effort to generate points toward the prize, our staff cranked out increased blog posts, tweets, and online comments; engaged in more sharing of ideas among and between client teams; participated in deeper levels of collaboration; and more. Even our customers commented on the great enthusiasm they sensed at Bluewolf.

Yes, it was costly to the company, but it more than paid for itself in myriad ways. Staff retention hit a record high. Employee morale, already high, grew even higher. Customer satisfaction rose substantially. Project volume and revenues increased. Our social gamification strategy proved such a success we're doing it again this year, drawing on internal feedback to improve the program and ensure we don't wind up in a rut.

Most important, our social strategy, through Prime, is inclusive of the entire company, regardless of the department where someone works. As an incentive program, it eclipses a typical "comp plan" that might be riddled with percentages or management by objectives (MBOs). Prime, as a social program, encourages collaboration and knowledge sharing at a level that breaks down the natural silos in our company, which is responsible for our positive metrics around retention and engagement.

USING SOCIAL

So, how do we use social besides gamification? We start with the use of Chatter, a Salesforce application. Chatter eliminates all the hassles of traditional e-mail and messaging and has changed the way we communicate. Gone are the mile-long message streams and blizzard of unrelated communications. Chatter enables our people to gather around initiatives and swarm around a customer to address one problem or another. It changes the way we function as an organization for the better.

But Chatter alone is not the end of our social story. Prime, noted earlier in regard to gamification, goes even further to facilitate collaboration and enhance our community environment. Rather than just extending our previous tool for marketing and brand awareness, Prime focuses on all aspects of working at Bluewolf. It aims to enhance the overall experience and provide opportunities for engagement for each employee, regardless of their role, all while keeping the customer as the center of attention.

Points are rewarded for a wide range of activities. These include social activities like blogging and social sharing as well as resource and client-focused activities like landing a new deal, creating a quality piece of content for our content library, teaching an internal Bluewolf class, or volunteering. Getting certified in Salesforce and partner technologies will generate even more points.

Probably the biggest part of Prime, however, is the recognition it allows for a job well done. We offer a series of badges that employees can award to each other to say thank you (see example in Figure 3.3). Sound trivial? Maybe so, but they work. The awards were designed to promote communication and expressions of gratitude for particularly helpful work or for

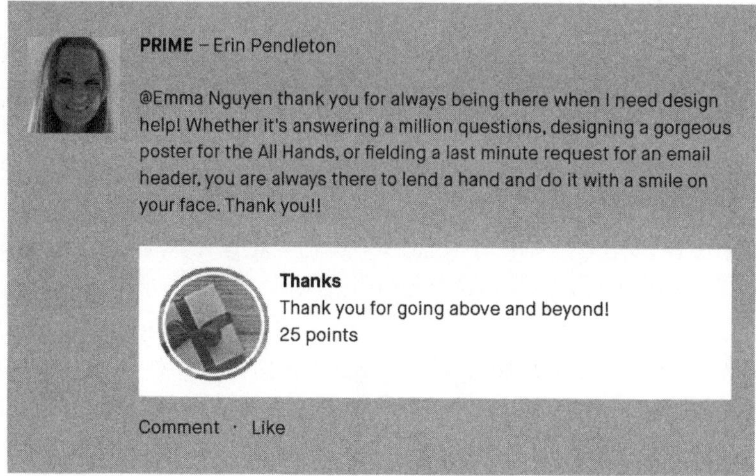

Figure 3.3 Example of Prime Thank-You Badge

contributing to the team in an unexpected way. In short, they were intended to enhance employee relationships and also assist in our employee review processes. During the self-assessment for performance reviews, employees can highlight the badges they have been awarded throughout the year to reinforce their assessment of the work they've completed. Employees have really embraced it; they make awards for each other, and those who receive the awards are genuinely appreciative. It actually does contribute to our high level of employee morale. And it simplifies and streamlines the annual employee review process, as well as contributes to increased employee retention. It also impacts customer relationships through more and better-engaged employees, which increases the customer's lifetime value at Bluewolf.

SOCIAL PAYBACK

Here is how I approach social at Bluewolf, and I recommend you approach it in the same way. Basically, social is a way to turn every employee, partner, stakeholder, and customer (yes, every customer, too) into an evangelist for what you do, a highly engaged advocate for your business. They do so, especially customers, because social enables you to give them a great experience as you deliver highly informed solutions that solve their problems.

This is possible with social because it gives you the means to know your customers extremely well and build specifically meaningful relationships with them. That enables you to anticipate customer needs, identify opportunities for the customer even before they do, and come up with appropriate solutions optimized specifically for that customer.

This isn't difficult. Just think about it. Customers go onto Facebook or Twitter or any social website and tell you specifically what they like and, most important, what they dislike. In the past, companies have had to spend a fortune surveying people and running focus groups to get the kind of insight people post on social websites every day, all day long, for free. All you have to do is collect it, think about it, and apply your creativity to help them achieve what they like and fix what they don't like. You don't even have to be a genius or a mind reader. The visitors tell you exactly what they like and don't like, often in brutally blunt ways.

The upshot: social gives you great opportunity to get to know your prospects and customers in surprising detail. Sure, there is all the superficial stuff, like sending birthday greetings or congratulations when some minor personal milestone or another has been reached, but that's not the high-value information. If you pay attention to what people post, you will quickly be able to discern the important stuff. Obviously, you want to jump on the gripes or complaints, respond quickly, and get them fixed. But also pay attention to the things people like, and figure out how you can do more of that. It can help build your customer base by attracting more like-minded people.

SOCIAL FOR CUSTOMER SERVICE

At Bluewolf, we treat social as much more than an alternative customer service channel, merely a way to bypass the call center. However, most organizations don't treat social that way, which is why I put this chapter prominently toward the front of the book. Early in 2015, Salesforce published some of its statistics on social for customer service. As I had hoped, Salesforce still makes a compelling case for social the way we use it here, which admittedly is not yet typical.

For example, in the United States, the cost of poor customer service amounts to $41 billion per year.[6] Don't fool yourself; even one poor customer service experience can spread like wildfire on social and turn off a lot of prospective customers. The bulk of customer service calls, 68 percent according to Salesforce (Figure 3.4), still come through the corporate call center, but 59 percent of 25- to 34-year-olds—those are marketers' hottest, most sought-after demographic—report they will share poor customer experiences online in a flash (Figure 3.5).

Social still isn't the first choice for customer service, but it has emerged as an extremely popular platform when it comes to sharing a bad experience. When people have a gripe, customers

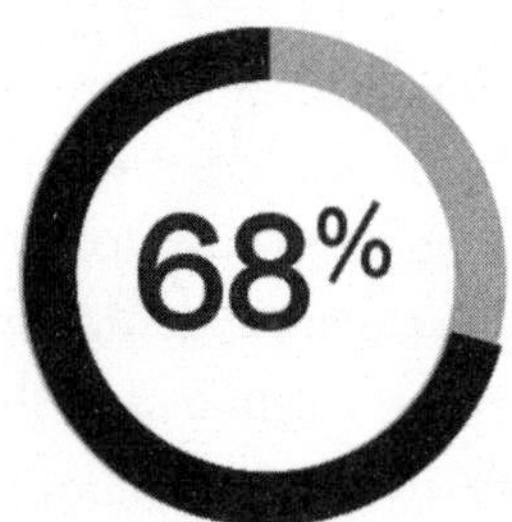

customer service calls still come through corporate call centers

Figure 3.4

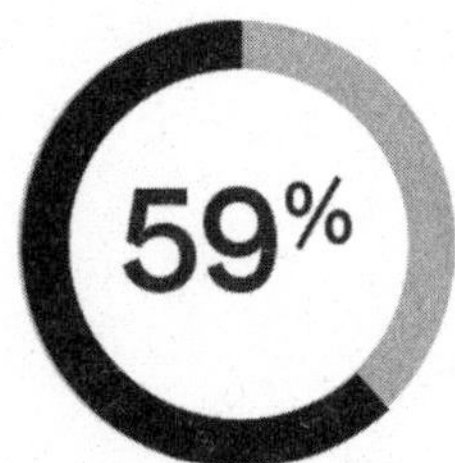

of 25–34 year olds report they will share poor customer experiences online in a flash

Figure 3.5

or not, they take their issue to social media. That's one reason we advise clients to monitor what is being said about them, bad or good, on social media and respond appropriately. Just think of Vodafone.

Obviously, the call center isn't going away, given that it continues to handle the bulk of all customer communications. As difficult as it is to find and retain good call center operators, even Salesforce recommends that organizations not neglect the tried-and-true phone call. Rest assured; if you do neglect phone calls, the resulting fury will show up first on social.

"Why?" asks Salesforce. Simple: as far as customers are concerned, it's often much easier to pick up the phone and speak to someone than it is to track a brand down on social media, although that may be a generational thing. At Bluewolf, we are picking up plenty of evidence that millennials prefer to resolve customer service issues directly on Twitter or Facebook, online chat, messaging, or even e-mail rather than via the phone.

In any case, at Bluewolf customers should have no problem contacting us via any channel. Whatever their position, we train all of our people to create, nurture, and sustain the customer or prospect relationship via social. In fact, they should have identified concerns, even the most minor ones, long before someone felt the need to complain. If someone has an issue and feels compelled to call us, we consider that a failure. Somebody here should have known of the issue early and had it satisfactorily resolved long before it got to that point.

Compared to call centers, social handles just 3 percent of all customer communications, reports Salesforce. At Bluewolf we handle much more via social. Just check out our numbers in the next section. Although most companies put their brands on social media, Facebook and Twitter are not yet the first channels of choice for consumers. At the rate they are growing, however, they might be before you know it. Facebook, for instance, is reporting over 1 billion members. That's about one-seventh of the population of the entire planet!

Before the Internet, if you upset a customer, three or four of their friends might know about it. In the twenty-first century, an upset customer can easily reach thousands of people within minutes. Providing good customer service is as much about maintaining your brand image as it is about your customer relationships. An unhappy customer complaining publicly is always bad for your brand.

Following a negative customer experience, Salesforce reports, 58 percent of Americans say they would never use that company again (Figure 3.6). That means that every time you fail to

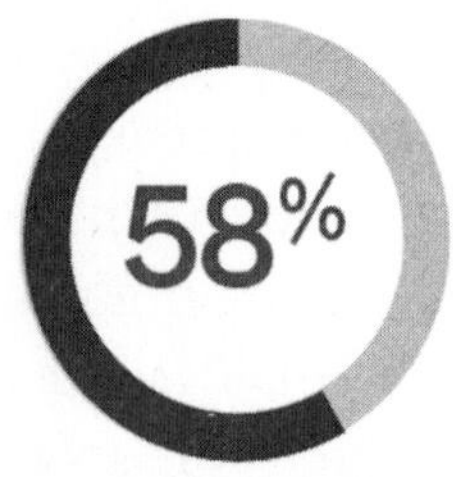

Figure 3.6

resolve a customer's issue satisfactorily, there's a better than 50 percent chance you'll never hear from them again. By nurturing relationships through social, you can shift this reaction more to your favor and ensure that your existing customers keep coming back.

Salesforce turned up some other interesting data worth noting here. For instance, failure to respond via social channels can lead to a 15 percent increase in customer churn. Social media might not yet be the most popular channel of communication, but it can have a big impact on how customers and prospective customers see your brand and how loyal they are. Failing to respond to someone is perhaps the absolute worst thing you could do—your customer will not only feel underappreciated and ignored, but their request will be left hanging on social media for all to see.

On the positive side, however, loyal customers are worth up to 10 times as much, on average, as their first purchase, according to Salesforce. That's the lifetime value of a customer, and social is a good way to cultivate it. Most businesses get too wrapped up in acquiring new customers—probably trying to offset customer churn due to poor service—which causes existing customers to feel neglected. Use social to nurture those customers by building a productive relationship they look forward to and participate in. Provide posts with especially relevant content or a solution to a problem—anything they will appreciate. When you do that they certainly won't feel ignored.

Finally, 60 percent of customers favor a balance of price and service and will no longer accept poor service in exchange for a cheap deal. Yes, in the early days of e-commerce, many shopped online in search of low prices and still do. But online business has become more than just low price—customers demand high-quality service, too. It is not an either-or situation; they want both or you will hear about it, probably via social.

BLUEWOLF'S SOCIAL PAYBACK

So how does Bluewolf stack up, especially in light of Salesforce's data? Our latest metrics show social overall driving 8 percent of the traffic to our website, up from 3–4 percent previously, and better than what Salesforce reports on average. In terms of other metrics, we've experienced:

Figure 3.7 Bluewolf Social Engagement Metrics

There also are some other gains we can attribute to social, including a notable increase in deal velocity and net new business leads, higher win rates, and more effective brand-building activities. When staff use social, for example, to collaborate around a customer opportunity, increasing customer satisfaction and producing a more effective solution faster, that's worth something, and it is measured through progress we see in shortened deal cycles, average revenue per sales rep, percentage of stalled projects, and amount of bad debt. Over time, this kind of problem solving leads to steady increases in the lifetime value of our customers' relationships with Bluewolf. When you come down to it, much of anything to do with an improved customer experience can be traced back to our use of social and the customer relationships that result.

Overall, we aim to take maximum advantage of social conversations to advance business goals. Social engagement boosts lifetime customer value, gives you an edge in intent-to-purchase conversations, and builds brand awareness and brand evangelists. Not only that, but it speeds deal velocity through highly responsive customer service and sustains and expands customer relationships, nurturing future sales.

So, in terms of social metrics, we have no serious complaints. Actually, more to the point, we are quite proud of what we have achieved with creating an ongoing social presence, proud enough to be willing to showcase how we do it in this chapter. That said, we're not so enamored with what we are doing as a company with social that we don't see room for improvement.

BUILDING A SOCIAL CULTURE IN YOUR ORGANIZATION

I previously laid out how Bluewolf uses social with the idea that you could use it or parts of it as a blueprint for your own social initiative. Please feel welcome to borrow whatever you like.

I am tempted to say it is fun to build a social culture in your organization since we started with gamification, but that may be a bit deceptive. While many parts of it *are* fun, you have to include all the serious management best practices you would use for any strategic business initiative. And don't kid yourself; this is indeed strategic, or at least it should be.

These best practices include having a purpose as the clear focus. You will rally your people around the purpose. You'll also want to articulate your vision and have a clear strategy along with goals to measure your progress toward success. This part is MBA Management 101, so you don't need to hear it from me.

The challenge of rolling out such a social program to connect your company both internally and externally provides plenty of issues to consider. In some ways, it's like raising teenagers. You know you have to give them more freedom, but how much and when? How do you guide their actions to a productive, positive conclusion without stifling their initiative?[7]

As I have noted from the start, technology isn't the problem. Technology platforms are readily available, and not just Salesforce—the real trick is getting people engaged and moving in a way that produces the desired results. If the company is global, often the first and perhaps biggest challenge is simply getting people talking to each other. Remember, people don't just spontaneously cross departmental, cultural, and geographical lines and freely communicate—you've got to make it happen and model the desired behavior. If management is not on social and actively engaging customers, coworkers, and partners, don't expect your staff to, either.

Here are a few tips for designing and implementing a social collaboration program that will move your organization forward.

Tip #1:

Know your team. When a platform becomes an abandoned amusement park (à la Myspace) or shelfware, it was most likely never finely tuned to the preferences of your people. If an enterprise social collaboration program is focused on anything but the people expected to use it, it will flounder.

You most likely have people in your organization and customer base who hail from India to Indiana, and all points in between. To further complicate things, you've probably got four generations working for you, ranging from people who learned math on an abacus to those who have used Google their entire lives and know nothing else. You will need to factor in the various cultures and generations represented by your workforce when it comes to devising and then implementing your social engagement plan. Since you will be throwing a lot at them to take in, it's best to start by establishing a baseline where your staff stands right now. Do this by determining:

- How active they are on the major social networks
- How much they understand about building their personal brand via the social web and what they feel about it

- What's holding them back from being more engaged (or engaged at all) in social media

Once you've got a grasp on these fundamentals, you'll have a solid footing to begin implementing a platform/program that leverages social media to engage your employees with your customers and with each other. If you want to add partners or associates, too (not required) simply use the same determinations for another set of people.

Tip #2:

Use enlightened self-interest. Many companies are beginning to understand the payoff of a successful social media program—improved customer care, collaboration, innovation, brand building, solving business problems faster, increased exposure, and so on. The problem is employees don't necessarily understand what's in it for them. Even if 100 percent of your workforce is using Facebook and Twitter incessantly, they may not see any benefit in using these tools in the professional realm, especially on behalf of their employer.

Motivating people to get socially engaged is different from other types of workplace motivation in that it has to be entirely positive. A poor attitude is a killer. Management may get away with cajoling employees into certain activities, like working a couple of hours later before a holiday, but you definitely don't want them amplifying their thoughts via social media with a bad attitude.

Instead, you've got to show them what's in it for them by leveraging the principle of enlightened self-interest. This philosophy, popularized by Adam Smith and leveraged during the framing of the U.S. government, holds that individuals seeking to improve their own station in life make better citizens and a better society. In the social media realm, if your top people are establishing themselves as subject experts online, this may equally benefit them as individuals and the company as a whole. With that in mind, be sure to reinforce the personal value to them of things that also serve the needs the organization, such as:

- Greater visibility to headhunters and prospective future employers
- Increased regard from your fellow workers and managers based on insightful or helpful comments
- Better visibility to the company's customers
- Increased recognition for your talents from all the above and whoever else stumbles upon you online

I can already hear readers saying: "No way. We can't allow this. All this increased visibility just makes them prey for headhunters." Don't worry: Everybody who is of interest to headhunters and competitors is already fully visible on Linkedin anyway. Your only bet is to make sure they don't want to leave. To revisit the teenager analogy, it's kind of like telling your kids they can't listen to certain popular music—they'll just do it anyway.

Tip #3:

Leverage plain old self-interest. If you were reading Tip #2 and thinking that it won't work for many of your people, you're probably right. Like teenagers, not everyone is motivated by long-term benefits, much less the company's greater good. If being hailed as an industry expert holds no allure, you may have to resort to instant gratification. Again, think dealing with teenagers. What could be more instantly gratifying than scoring points in a game? For many organizations, gamifying social media engagement may prove a very effective tactic as it can inspire people to take action, even those who otherwise might have zero interest in participating. We have parlayed games and contests, referred to as gamification at Bluewolf, into a variety of desired results.

Companies are using game mechanics to boost performance in all kinds of functions, particularly sales, and the same principles can be applied to social media participation. For example, you can offer incentives for posting your company's content, and even greater incentives if that content sparks a lively online discussion or gets retweeted.

So how do you build an engaging, gamified user experience around your social enterprise rollout? One way is to make the technology serve people, not the other way around. This holds doubly true in the realm of social media, which many companies are leveraging to connect globally dispersed workforces and clients.[8] This sounds ridiculously apparent, but since the dawn of the PC era people have been conditioned to serve the technology. Take the opportunity to implement a social business strategy to break down this worthless fixture from the past.

CIOs implementing platforms that facilitate enterprise-wide collaboration face the same challenge they face every time they roll out any new application or system—engagement. You may be tempted to think giving your people the tools would be incentive enough. After all, you're offering them a chance to essentially mimic their spare-time behaviors. However, assuming they're going to engage with your social tools just because they use Facebook is like thinking they'll watch company videos because they like to watch TV. In reality, if you don't totally wrap the experience around their preferences and needs, you'll have no more luck getting them to use your tools than you would trying to get them to watch a really bad TV series.

Reasons for disengagement may be as varied as your employees themselves—too slammed, not sure how to get started, unclear about the rules, don't have anything worth sharing, don't really care—the list goes on. The bottom line is that you may have to do quite a bit of coaxing and hand holding to get things moving. A late afternoon party offering free pizza and beer and revolving around a social business activity or event could periodically energize the troops. Of course, you could also build some gamification contests around it.

Let's start with this premise: It is in the organization's best interests to make a good social strategy work. In the long run it benefits everybody. Now, what can you do to bring your people onboard?

MAKE IT EASY

Make it easier than "liking" a video of a cat falling into the toilet. To succeed, your people have to view this as fun, and the bar for that has been set pretty high on the consumer side (you've got people sharing epic fails, dogs doing tricks, and don't even get me started on the cat videos). Aside from offering an attractive platform, you must make it easy. How easy? Easy enough that someone who feels they don't have enough time to take a lunch break will think it an effortless task to share a piece of company content through a social channel. If you haven't read Steve Krug's book on website design, *Don't Make Me Think*, check it out. He describes exactly what I mean.

Using game dynamics to drive adoption can be a very effective tactic, but I caution you to make the game as effortless as possible—think *Angry Birds*, not *Call of Duty*. For example, if you're offering points for someone to post a company blog through a social channel, you should also consider implementing functionality that both feeds content to them that they're likely to find personally compelling and enables them to post to multiple accounts with one or two clicks.

LIGHT THE WAY

Show them the light. Even employees who completely get the value of your program and have every intention of engaging with it may not know where to start. They may be totally fluent in social media, yet unsure how to engage on behalf of your company. For that matter, the idea of using social media for a concrete goal may be completely foreign. You have to train them by providing convenient, free training on the company's time, not their personal time.

Don't, however, make the mistake of sending your team to some off-site seminar on "how to be social." One allure of social media is how it melds into other aspects of our lives—social media training should be no different. Research is beginning to show that the most effective learning is informal—that is, training that your team can take in bite-sized chunks while on the go, through a variety of platforms and delivery methods (videos, SlideRockets, Prezi presentations, and so on). In general, anything lasting more than five minutes is going to fall flat in this age of waning attention spans and constant interruption.

ITERATE AND REFINE

Don't give up on the cat video devotees. Aim for 100 percent adoption, but don't make it your immediate goal. A few months in, gauge who is participating and who isn't, and iterate your plan to get stragglers on board.

For example, while you're going to see plenty of people engaged in the program that you fully anticipated would be early adopters, were there any surprises? Were there any team members who caught fire contrary to your expectations? If so, find out what did it for them, and try to leverage that success to get others on board. Better yet, recruit them as evangelists to the cause, even if you have to come up with more free pizza and beer.

Conversely, is there someone you were sure would be your star evangelist who has so far failed to engage? Maybe someone who incessantly posts photos of their cat dressed up like Batman, yet hasn't retweeted a single company-related comment? If so, do your homework and find out why they're not engaged, and what would make it both fun and worthwhile for them.

BUILDING AN EXTERNAL SOCIAL PRESENCE

If you've heard me speak at Dreamforce, you know I tend to focus on the high-level stuff. My technical team doesn't want me straying into the nitty-gritty details that I haven't done personally for years and might get wrong. And much of this chapter so far has been pretty high level, too.

But let's take a moment to drop down a little to discuss how you actually go about building an external social presence for your company. Creating an engaging, customer-facing social persona intended to attract hundreds, thousands, even tens of thousands of followers for your business can be quite a bit different than building an internal social culture. You can't exactly throw a pizza and beer party for all of the people you'd like to have follow your company on Twitter and LinkedIn. So, you will have to do something different. Specifically, the most effective way to engage customers on social is to do the following:

- Do your research and know your audience. Just like any other marketing campaign, you have to understand who you're trying to reach and what you'd like to achieve, be it more likes, retweets, or lead conversions.
- While you are setting goals for your business's social persona, be a little more ambitious. Shoot beyond likes. Try to

get people to comment, pose appropriate and relevant questions to generate some answers, and post provocative (but not controversial) ideas people can comment on. The idea is to get a response or start a dialogue.

- Have a consistent message communicated through diverse content. Social is a huge opportunity to amplify your brand, but you need an interesting message, hopefully even a compelling one, to start. Then you need to stay on message while engaging your audience with useful, thoughtful content.
- Don't be afraid to engage people directly. Many companies fall into the trap of scheduling social posts to promote their business but don't respond to messages, mentions, and hashtags. They miss out on a prime opportunity to connect with their customers in a very real, very personal way.
- Organic growth on social is great, but don't neglect paid promotion, either. Use your customer knowledge to target the right audience and design ads and sponsored posts to draw them into your social engagement circle.
- Finally, and this is one that falls in line with an internal tactic, use self-interest to get your customers to promote you. Host giveaways and contests to boost your customers' interest and involvement with your brand.

None of this is difficult or expensive, but it does require time and thoughtful effort. No one can build a social media empire overnight—even Kim Kardashian didn't begin with a million followers. It is worth investing in a team member whose sole focus is managing and promoting your brand via social. Cultivate your best content creators to drive consistent and increased traffic and engagement with your brand. If you get visitors to come back to your social page, you've won! Now keep them coming back with useful news, thought leadership, and personal engagement.

BENEFITS OF BUILDING A SOCIAL CULTURE

Here are three big benefits that accrue to a company with an active and engaged social culture:

1. Engaged workers who are out evangelizing for the company and its brands
2. Satisfied, loyal customers who are happily engaged with the company and its staff
3. An enviable social presence that builds brand value and attracts more customers without being intrusive or off-putting

In the process of building up the first three benefits, you actually acquire a fourth benefit, which is equally valuable although it may be more ephemeral—positive social capital. In short, you have social goodwill that may help save your reputation if something bad happens, like a database hack that compromises personal data. Of course you will have to do everything possible to correct both the problem and mitigate the negative fallout, but your reservoir of social goodwill may soften the worst blowback and keep you in business.

SOCIAL MEDIA ROI

There are so many ways an effective social program contributes a return on investment (ROI). Here are a few that immediately come to mind:

1. Saves time and speeds processes, especially customer-oriented processes
2. Reduces overhead—maybe this is the result of number one, but here it is nonetheless

3. Increases customer and employee retention
4. Increases sales efficiency—how much does it cost to acquire and keep a customer?
5. Expands customer relationships and increase lifetime value, including upsell and cross-sell
6. Drives organic growth—growth that you cultivate and nurture internally and externally
7. Fuels innovation—by making it easy to share ideas
8. Enables efficient collaboration—see #7
9. Enhances brand appeal, profitability, and efficiency

I can't tell you the specific ROI Bluewolf has achieved from its social initiatives, but I can tell you this: our marketing budget grows at a slower rate than our revenue. Why? Because our social programs have tapped into latent, and free, knowledge in our organization that would otherwise stay internal and need to be recreated through traditional marketing efforts. Social, through something like our Prime program, taps into deep organizational knowledge and exposes it to our customers. It minimizes the refraction that typically happens when a marketing or sales organization attempts to communicate the benefits of a product or service.

I once had a conversation with someone at a Nike store and asked them about a specific running shoe. That person spoke of the features of the shoe at a high level. It sounded like the pitch for any running shoe I have ever looked at. But then the sales rep walked me to a video console and clicked on a simple YouTube video. On it, this particular shoe's designer spoke of its merits while holding it in her hand. She went deeper than any well-trained sales rep could ever go. The video was a little raw. She held the shoe in her hand. She held up a drawing of the shoe's design. Most important, she spoke passionately about it. She truly believed this shoe was best suited for a 45-year-old man with creaky knees. I bought the shoe. That knowledge was free to Nike. And it created engagement beyond what any marketing department could ever recreate.

One last point: The hardest part of social business is sustaining it and keeping it fresh. This is a constant creative challenge, and one I lose a certain amount of sleep over. Social business and your visitors are changing constantly. You never want to allow your social culture to go stale.

This really means keeping your content—your posts and tweets and blogs and any other content—fresh, engaging, and above all, current. Like social itself, your customers and other stakeholders are changing all the time, and they expect you to keep up. You want your social audience to always find something new, something interesting. It doesn't have to be earthshaking, just different. At Bluewolf we probably refresh various content a dozen times a day, often little more than a few new tweets. People here earn gamification points for doing it, which motivates them to come up with new material periodically. The goals of the effort are to keep your audience coming back and to keep them excited about your company and what you are doing. Yes, it takes time and effort, but you don't need that much new material to keep your social experience fresh. The cost, actually, can be quite minimal, but the payback will be more than worth it.

4

Rethinking Employee Engagement

UNIFYING A DIVERSE TEAM

It seems self-evident that diversity is good for beauty companies given that they want to sell hair coloring, skin care, and other beauty aids to women of every ethnic makeup. To that end, one of Bluewolf's recent clients (anonymized for privacy) issued its first diversity report at the end of 2015 noting inclusion of people with disabilities and, most important, inclusion of people of diverse social and ethnic origins. In the report, the company's chairman and CEO declared that the "management of diversity is a strategic lever for us. A diverse workforce in all functions and levels of a company enhances our creativity and our understanding of consumers, thus allowing us to develop and market products that are relevant to their expectations."

When it comes to diversity, this beauty industry company is actually looking beyond its direct staff. It is cultivating a cadre of independent hairstylists and colorists who will teach customers and others the techniques and use of their products. Once women all over the world understand how best to use hair coloring and makeup and other beauty aids for their skin, hair color, and personal tastes, they will be more likely to not only buy this company's products but buy the *right* products and be more satisfied with the results.

To me, this sounded like a great strategy. There was only one catch: the company needed tools that would help this large and diverse workforce, not all of whom were direct employees, access the same information. They were already off to a good start, but needed some improvements. They had a digital sales aid from Salesforce, but they weren't happy with it. To begin, it only did content management and even then, it wasn't integrated with data.

The company also needed the tool to support its growing community of what it referred to as "hair artists," elite hairstylists, about 1,000 worldwide, who teach classes and show how best to use company products. These are not direct employees, but freelancers who teach their products to the women around the world who will buy and use them.

Unfortunately, their hair artists were running about 200 functions in a given week. This was far too much to handle, especially when many of those instructors weren't even the company's own people. So, we created an app to make it easier to use those core functionalities, and we mobilized it so the instructors could run it on their smartphones.

The results were exactly as we intended. Sales reps are getting the latest info on the customer before they make the call. Also, inputting data into the system is much easier and the resulting reporting, too, has become much better. Finally, the independent elite hair colorists can easily get the info they need to appropriately guide their customers on the best use of the company's products.

WORKERS MATTER TO SUCCESS

This beauty company's experience proves an often overlooked issue: your workers, whether direct employees or not, matter to

1/3 **of companies cite an employee-facing initiative as one of their top three priorities in 2016**

Figure 4.1 The State of Salesforce 2015–2016

the success of your business initiatives. You need to cultivate this incredibly valuable yet overlooked asset. Such assets are overlooked because management often takes them for granted; we're paying them, so they will do what we say. This chapter will show how wrong that assumption actually is.

Even within the Salesforce community, employees are clearly attracting new attention. In the latest Bluewolf State of Salesforce Report, 2015, one-third of the companies cite an employee-facing initiative as one their top three priorities for 2016 (Figure 4.1). That goes hand-in-hand with other data from the study showing companies are three times more likely to attribute measurable business outcomes to the use of tools that make the jobs of their employees easier. Now it seems employees have become prime targets for the deployment of advanced technology. I consider that a major step forward.

It wasn't always so. I remember when companies employed one of two approaches toward their workforce:

- Old way: Employees were generally regarded as unthinking cogs who did as managers directed. Discipline was rigid, there were few incentives for initiative or creativity, and, maybe most telling, employees had no input. Okay, maybe a little in rare organizations, but by and large, managers dictated the way the game was played and employees were expected to be happy they had a decent job.

- Compare this to today—now employees in many organizations are empowered to take action, show initiative, make decisions, and generally engage their minds. Collaborative initiatives are welcome, employee input is seriously considered, and companies award appropriate incentives for actions that advance the organization's goals.

Clearly, we are witnessing a significant evolution in the workplace and among the workforce. Maybe it's not happening everywhere, at least not yet, but this evolution is already under way. And you should expect it to continue and build momentum going forward. The workplace and the workforce are definitely changing fast.

The change can't come fast enough for companies that intend to succeed. The Gallup organization has been collecting the largest body of behavioral economic data in the world on workplace trends. Its singular conclusion: *miserable employees create miserable customers.*[1] The author, Jim Clifton, chairman and CEO of Gallup, puts the result in terms of the Six Sigma quality language around defects. (In case you missed it, Six Sigma was a response to Japanese quality gains in manufacturing a couple of decades ago and is still in practice in many businesses today.)

To translate Gallup's conclusions into Six Sigma terms, Clifton writes: "A miserable employee, particularly a miserable manager, is a defect—a defect for the company and for the customer."[2] A defect in Six Sigma thinking must be avoided at all costs.

Clifton's book really focuses on the creation of what he considers good jobs at the macroeconomic level, but in the process he points out some smart things about handling workers on the immediate day-to-day business level. For example, he refers to extremely miserable employees as actively disengaged, actively because they encourage coworkers to disengage as well. Bluewolf is not a Six Sigma operation, but we strive to have

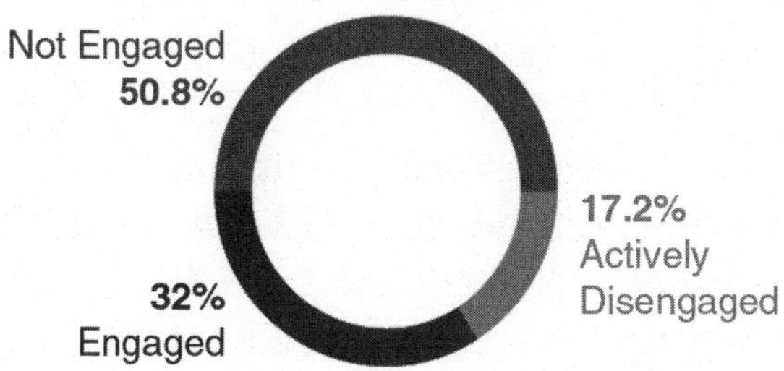

Figure 4.2 Gallup Employee Engagement Statistics, 2015

satisfied, productive employees who are fully engaged, the exact opposite of Clifton's actively disengaged worker.

In the book, Clifton identifies three types of workers: engaged, not engaged, and actively disengaged. If you are striving to deliver an exceptional customer experience, you want engaged employees. For those not currently engaged, you can turn to gamification and other techniques to engage them. Lastly, you need to identify and replace the actively disengaged employees as quickly as possible before they infect your engaged workers and, worse still, degrade the customer experience for your customers. To give you a sense of employee engagement across the United States, see Figure 4.2.

EMPLOYEE ENGAGEMENT (OR LACK THEREOF) AND PRODUCTIVITY

Gallup estimates that 50.8 percent of the U.S. workforce is not engaged; not actively *dis*engaged, mind you, but still not engaged. You know them and probably work with them, suggests Clifton. They have no concern about customers, productivity, profitability, waste, safety, mission, or the purpose of the team. Mainly, they are thinking about lunch or their next break. Surprisingly, these aren't just the obvious goof-offs. Some, Clifton points out, may be sitting on your executive committee.

Then there are the actively disengaged employees. According to Gallup, they have more on-the-job accidents, cause more quality defects, and contribute to theft, euphemistically referred to as shrinkage, all of which cost the organization. In the process, they are sicker, miss more days, and quit at a higher rate. In short, they just add up to more and higher costs. Says Clifton, "When you are in a meeting with nine other people, odds are that two of them are taking notes to make damn sure whatever you're planning doesn't see light of day."[3] Next time you're sitting in a meeting, see if you can identify the actively disengaged coworkers.

That leaves the remaining 30 percent—your engaged employees. They are the builders of the organization and the creative force behind everything good that happens in the company. And, something particularly dear to me at Bluewolf, "they are the only people in your organization who create new customers."[4] (Keep Gallup's employee classification in mind when we get to Stan Slap's discussion of your employee culture later.)

Gallup calculates that "if twice as many American workers scored high on its frames of mind quiz it would create sudden significant change; it would generate more rapid job growth than anything else."[5] It would also double innovation and double entrepreneurship.

The best of these employees, not surprisingly, have higher customer metrics, higher productivity, and higher profitability. Expectedly, they also have lower absenteeism, lower turnover, less theft, fewer accidents, and fewer quality defects, ranging from 25 to 60 percent less.

Employee engagement, to me, is more predictive of a company's success than almost any other independent factor. If your employees are not engaged, you can bet your customers aren't either.

Understanding Employee Culture—Critical to Business Success

Are you aware of your organization's employee culture? Can you describe it in a few key phrases or a sentence or two? If you can't, then ask a few employees to describe the employee culture and hope they will be at least a little bit frank with you. Understanding your employee culture is critical to increasing the amount of engaged employees working for you, moving the not engaged to engaged, and weeding out the actively disengaged.

Every organization with employees has an employee culture. As a manager, figuring it out is not always straightforward, and it can shift as the organization changes, especially as things shift in the executive and middle to uppermanagerial ranks. But there are constants you can be sure of with any employee culture. By the way, theoretically managers, too, could be part of the employee culture, but don't fool yourself; there are limits to how accepted even a low or midlevel manager will be.

In addition to constantly observing you, the manager, your employee culture is focused on security, self-protection, and predictability. Security could be immediate job security or a more generalized security revolving around the future of the company. Self-protection deals with concerns about the reasonableness or arbitrary nature of management decisions. Predictability is also related to the arbitrary nature of company decision making. Will unexpected decisions pull the rug out from under anyone or everyone? The employee culture is highly tuned to this question in the most nuanced way. Stan Slap, a noted business management consultant and author of *Under the Hood*, a book exploring employee culture, writes: "Your customers are employees somewhere, too, so they belong to the overall employee culture. They will protect or reject your company in part based on how they perceive your company treats people just like themselves."[6]

What this means is that contrary to whatever you learned in grad school earning that shiny MBA, you are not going to have control. You don't have control until the employee culture temporarily grants some measure of it to you. If you haven't figured this out yet, heed the wise words of Stan Slap: "If your employee culture wants something to happen in your business, it will. If it doesn't, it won't."[7]

The employee culture is always wary, highly skeptical, and constantly monitoring your every move and those of every other manager to collect the smallest, most nuanced bits of information to sift and analyze and decide whether or not to play along, how much, and how enthusiastically. It will decide hour by hour, even minute by minute how credible and trustworthy you are. With every utterance and action, your credibility is at stake.

Slap still says it best: "An employee culture exists to protect itself. . . . It is an information gathering organism, designed to ensure its own survival."[8] Expect the employee culture to resist change and drag its feet until it has been thoroughly convinced. Although it is possible to win over the employee culture, at least temporarily, it can be lost in an instant, too. All it takes is one decision that contradicts what you say. Imply that a decision you want implemented will not result in any layoffs and then lay off a few people and you are toast. To paraphrase Monopoly, don't pass go and don't collect $200. The best you can do is to start trying to build credibility all over again—just don't blow it this time.

You can win over the employee culture and enlist it to execute change. Per Slap's advice, it will take honest, full disclosure of what is and is *not* changing. Try to arrange what is not changing to be recognizably greater than what is changing. Then embark on a 90-day path to get there, preferably in small steps, and "light the unknown road ahead a little bit at a time—as if you were holding a lantern down the darkened path, allowing the culture to see far enough ahead to proceed at least that far with confidence."[9] Employee culture, change averse in most cases to begin with, is not likely to embrace a big bang approach to new initiatives. If you have to do something like that, prepare it well in advance, telegraph every move, and then do it exactly as you laid it out.

Case for Employee Engagement

You've already learned that some types of employees can damage your business, especially customer relationships—a vital priority—and new strategic initiatives. Every employee relationship incurs monetary and nonmonetary overhead that must be addressed in one way or another. Even your best employees create headaches; they have lives, which can impact the business in big or small ways. They can have a sick child, be going through a divorce, or be dealing with an aging parent; situations like these invariably impact their work and, consequently, the business. Such things happen to everyone, and must be considered as part of the normal employee overhead. And I haven't even started to list the personal foibles and such that can disrupt the workplace. As a manager, you just have to be prepared to make whatever adjustments and accommodations are necessary to keep productivity high and the workplace operating smoothly.

That said, it is always best, within reason, to accommodate the human shortcomings that will assuredly upset your best workforce plans. There are a variety of good reasons for this, starting with these two:

- Keeping a productive worker going through a rough patch is easier and cheaper than finding and training a replacement and waiting for them to become productive.
- The need to maintain the value of customer engagement and those employee relationships can be critical. We have talked about the lifetime value of customer relationships, but

there is also the lifetime value of a productive employee and the employee's role in customer satisfaction. Think about it.

Up to this point, I've only been talking about good employees. The cost of nonengaged employees or actively disengaged employees presents an entirely different problem. According to Gallup, actively disengaged employees—the least productive—cost the American economy up to $350 billion per year in lost productivity.[10] Some slice of that is coming directly out of your pocket and impacting your bottom line.

How bad is the situation? Let's recap Gallup's engagement statistics. According to Gallup, only 32 percent of the U.S. workforce is actively engaged. Of the remainder, 50.8 percent are not engaged and 17.2 percent are actively disengaged, which Gallup identified as a costly defect that you want to minimize and then remove.

After analyzing the survey data, Gallup came up with two rules managers can count on:

1. Employee engagement = customer engagement. Which, by the way, is the gospel here at Bluewolf.
2. The best predictor of sales growth is employee engagement.

That should tell you why, along with customer experience, now is the time to elevate employee experience to a comparable level.

Employee-Facing Initiatives

The simple reality today is that companies don't place enough emphasis on the employee experience. Too often, the employee experience is at the bottom of the corporate priority list, despite being such an important predictor of customer engagement and sales growth.

That mind-set, however, seems to be changing. In our latest State of Salesforce Report, one-third of the companies named an employee-facing initiative as one of their top three objectives in 2016.

Company management is finally getting it; they now understand that investing in employees is an investment in a company's bottom line. The place to begin is to improve the overall employee experience by first simplifying time-consuming tasks. This will enable your employees to spend more time with customers.

Managing your company employee and management culture is your next task. This is not just a mission statement. Rather, it lays out a set of beliefs that shape how you interact with and support your employees and support your brand promise. While you're at it, remember to keep faith with whatever you have promised to the employee culture.

According to Stan Slap, that means, first and foremost, being consistent in good times and bad. The first thing employees look for is whether these values go out the window in times of stress. The number one critical mistake you can make is to ignore, abuse, or violate commitments as perceived by the employee culture.

Employee Heaven or Pressure Cooker

A few companies have a vision for the kind of employee experience they want and act on it. Netflix, the online video-streaming giant, certainly is one. It has created a unique and, to many, an enviable employee experience. Netflix employees have unlimited vacation, expense without manager oversight, and don't have regular performance reviews.

A few years ago, many people reasonably questioned how long Netflix might survive. Its industry—film and video distribution—was in upheaval. It needed to convert millions of customers from its old delivery model, which relied on physical DVDs sent via the mail, to a new online streaming model. It also needed to navigate a change in pricing and its pricing model, which it initially bungled.

Now the company has emerged as the poster child for the modern cloud-based innovative company. Its streaming platform is the envy of many, and its customer base is heading into the stratosphere (by the end of 2014 it had over 69 million streaming subscribers and was still growing).[11]

Its employee experience certainly is attracting attention, although there haven't been reports of other large companies flocking to adopt it in full. At Bluewolf, we have borrowed ideas from the Netflix approach. For example, we share common values like embracing and encouraging autonomy. We're also open to employee-led initiatives and ideas and a flexible vacation policy. But we still have midyear and annual reviews, although those aren't necessarily focused on culling the herd. We actually work hard to retain employees. I'm not saying we don't let people go when their performance is subpar, but our primary focus is on employee enablement and retention.

One thing I particularly like about the Netflix employee experience is their cultural transparency and how they actively seek employees who affirm and contribute to it. At Bluewolf, we understand the importance of a mutual cultural fit, especially when it comes to teamwork and workplace camaraderie.

That said, the Netflix approach isn't ideal for everybody. It puts a lot of pressure on employees to perform in an environment that appears to have no limits. Sure, they can take vacations when they want, but is that time off truly relaxing? I wonder how many of their high achievers take tablets and laptops with them on vacation and respond to e-mail? If you know, clue me in.

CREATING A HIGH-ENERGY, CUSTOMER-AWARE, EMPLOYEE-DRIVEN WORKPLACE

The real question becomes: how can you build a customer-aware, employee-driven workplace? The trick is to use your employees to influence those who can impact your target customers. It's actually not as hard as it may seem. Here are six steps to get you started:

1. Build a social-powered collaborative workplace.
2. Encourage your employees to own innovation in the workplace.
3. Leverage gamification to influence and stimulate employee behavior.
4. Empower all employees to own the customer moment.
5. Ensure employees have a stake and a voice.
6. Make sure employees know how and why their work is important and how it contributes to the overall customer experience.

The last point is the most important. Every employee should own the customer moment and understand how each encounter adds to or detracts from the customer experience. Obviously, you want to make sure it adds to the customer experience. To that end, set up systems to make it is easy for your teams to collaborate with each other and with customers. There are many systems to do this; we use Salesforce and Chatter, but there are others out there.

Beyond that, encourage diversity of people and ideas. It's surprising how often managers work hard to set up a racially or gender-diverse workforce, but forget about diversity of ideas. If everybody thinks the same way, you won't get unique ideas, which are critical for innovation. Proactively source diverse talent and ensure projects are staffed by a variety of employees. Otherwise employees, if given the choice, are likely to gravitate toward projects with like-minded people. And there goes the value of diversity.

Ensure managers know they are responsible for the makeup of your organization; actively work with them to ensure that diverse perspectives are well represented. This isn't to avoid the ire of the PC police. Diversity breeds creativity and better problem solving, and that is what this really is all about. You can best accomplish this by setting the example with an open-door policy.

It also helps to encourage a culture of helpfulness. Employees must feel comfortable reaching out to coworkers for help, regardless of team or project. You can use gamification to reinforce these behaviors and reward helpfulness as you saw in the previous chapter. Similarly, use gratitude and appreciation to reinforce and reward desired behavior. As previously noted, even a simple thank-you can go very far in this regard.

Finally, you want to encourage sociability. That doesn't sound very productive at all, more like just hanging around the water cooler. As it turns out, it is more productive than you can imagine.

Super Chicken

Ever hear about the super chicken? It became a legendary TED talk video you must watch.[12] In the video, presenter Margaret Heffernan looks at what makes some teams more successful than others. This is a problem with which every manager wrestles. For decades, we have believed that team success is tied to superstars. Superstars win sports championships and the Super Bowl, superstar programmers build awesome new innovative products, and on and on. Well, the super chicken experiment proved that wrong.

In the super chicken experiment, researchers took a normal group of chickens and watched their productivity over a number of generations, measuring productivity by the number of eggs each chicken laid. After a period of time, they separated the very best egg producers—your all-star chickens or super chickens. These were put into their own group. The researchers counted the egg productivity of the super chickens and compared it to the normal group. They expected the super chicken group to greatly outproduce the normal group. They were surprised to discover super chicken productivity did not surpass the normal group but was shockingly dismal. As it turns out, the top super chickens pecked the others in the super chicken group to distraction or even death. They were aggressive, disruptive, wasteful, and worked to suppress the rest—sort of like Gallup's actively disengaged workers. These super chickens weren't just sitting on their eggs, but were actively disrupting any productive efforts of the other chickens in the super chicken group.

The lesson here (I will resist the temptation to say don't count your chickens until they hatch) is to *not* count on superstars to carry your team. Subsequent research (not among chickens but human teams) showed the most success came to teams that were characterized by empathy and social sensitivity to one another. The best teams, it turns out, were those that shared the most social connectedness among the members of the team. Maybe our grandmothers were right all along about being nice, sharing, and playing well with others. As it turns out, those traits will indeed produce the most successful teams. As for the lone wolves and superstars—leave them to do their own things and tap them only when you really need their special talents. Better still, focus on recruiting talented, team-oriented, and collaborative employees.

How can any author follow the super chicken example? Instead, I will just rattle off, admittedly at risk of sounding like your mother, the remaining important things to consider or do to create a successful team:

- Engage your direct reports regularly. You cannot facilitate teamwork and collaboration if you are kept in the dark about their initiatives and progress.
- Improve the employee experience to improve the customer experience.

- Use employee shadowing to baseline and measure improvement. (Employee shadowing is a technique where you spend a day right alongside an employee for the purpose of learning how he or she works and how you can help.)

Truthfully, there is no magic secret to improving the employee experience. You have to invest both time and money to ensure an excellent employee experience. That takes many forms, such as personal attention, creativity, sincere interest, good tools, and more along the same lines. Anything that comes from you as a manager, be it information, a compliment, or personal connection, takes on heightened value and importance. Remember, the employee culture is constantly monitoring managers for any signs that may address their key concerns. Yes, you are living in a fishbowl. If that's the case, try to take advantage of it to reinforce your bridges to, and credibility with, the employee culture. It will pay dividends in many ways, often when and how you least expect it.

STRATEGIES TO IMPROVE THE EMPLOYEE EXPERIENCE

A great employee experience demands more than great vacation perks. Your employees value investments in training, tools, and their well-being. Here are some additional tactics and tips to get you started:

- Invest in ongoing training and credible communication.
- Provide appropriate and modern tools.
- Think mobile-first—your priority should be making your employees' jobs easier. Enable your workers with mobile tools, data, and applications to keep them up to speed and on track.

- Express appreciation, both verbally and experientially. Employees who feel valued show it through their work, their customer interaction, and how they speak about their job to outside friends and family.
- Create a culture of feedback and transparency.
- Give honest, consistent evaluation to take the guesswork out of performance evaluation.

Above all else, keep employees informed—doubts like "Will I get my bonus?" or "Am I getting promoted?" can reduce employee effectiveness to the point where it begins to impact the customer experience. It is easy to avoid simply by keeping people informed.

Employee Engagement Has a Direct Impact on Your Profitability

The more engaged your employees are, the more efficient and productive they will be and the more successful you will be. In the same way, digital cannot and should not be your only avenue for building up a positive employee culture and experience in your organization. Don't underestimate the power of face-to-face communication between coworkers and managers/employees. That's why there are pizza and beer gatherings on Friday afternoons.

However, not everything has to be a pizza and beer social. Host events in the office, line up professional development classes, set up off-site summits—anything to get your employees together. Such contact, professionally and socially, is invaluable in building bonds between your employees and creating goodwill and trust toward management and the company itself. And don't forget to include your customers at some of these events.

International Data Corporation's recent Experience Survey 2015 stated "the ability to link both employee and customer experiences together in order to deliver a holistic view of digital and social transformation is at the epicenter of competitive differentiation."[13] While enterprises must approach their business strategy through a customer-obsessed lens, they cannot successfully drive digital transformation or create unique customer moments if their employees are unmotivated and bogged down by old, clunky technology. These factors hinder their ability to engage with customers and excel at their jobs.

Companies need to put more accountability, authority, and information into the hands of employees who are closest to their products and customers. When employees have access to tools that improve the quality of their work lives, they can service clients in the moment. Businesses that provide opportunities that incentivize and reward this important work also reduce the barriers that prevent deeper engagement at work and with customers.

Let's end this discussion with this simple fact: 69.4 percent of companies are designed around a common goal: improving their business by elevating both the employee and customer experiences. Companies that invest in deepening that engagement through well-defined strategies will ultimately reap long-term benefits that are felt throughout the organization and seen through measurable business results.

5

Customer Engagement Defined

The mission of any state's Department of Labor is to help the state's economy thrive. As part of that mission, the department handles and processes all unemployment insurance claims in the state.

Unfortunately for one particular eastern state's citizen claimants, that department's antiquated legacy systems housed an incomplete data set that led to unusually slow handling of unemployment insurance appeals. The system not only lacked important data about the appellant and the related case details but was also missing a record of agent activity. As a result, the unemployment insurance appeals backlog had reached more than 18,000 cases, and the average time for processing an appeal had shot up to 189 days, which forced many of their citizens to go months without unemployment insurance or due process of their case.

To make matters worse, the U.S. Department of Labor (US DOL) imposes time-lapse regulations when doling out money to states for unemployment programs. Because of its delays, the state was in jeopardy of losing federal funding. If nothing else, state leadership needed a way to help the staff stay in compliance with US DOL statutes regarding the response time on the appeals.

Bluewolf was convinced it could modernize the unemployment claims processing and improve the technical processes to better serve the people of the state, which happened to include some Bluewolf employees (although not among the laid-off benefits claimants). We worked with the department to implement Salesforce Service Cloud, delivering an improved digital and connected experience for their citizens.

Specifically, we replaced the department's legacy system with a proprietary Salesforce FullForce certified solution called Bluewolf AppealsTrak. AppealsTrak automates every step of the appeals process from case intake and preparation, to appearance scheduling, decision tracking, and reporting. Batch printing through Conga Composer has streamlined decision making and communication; prescriptive data workflows have automated case prioritization; and data quality controls have massively reduced duplicate data in the system, which ensures accurate records and reporting. Better still, the new solution was built and deployed in only 16 weeks with widespread adoption. No shelfware here.

Now, the department's employees have an easily configurable and scalable solution to serve the needs of its citizens and to ensure due process. State leadership has the visibility and insight it needs to successfully guide and advise staff on all US DOL Statues, and the state provides the US DOL with an accurate time-lapse standards report as proof of its compliance.

Citizens of that state are now experiencing timely processing of unemployment appeals, providing them with their rightful compensation when they lose their jobs. A little more than a year out from our engagement, the department has eliminated its user backlog. The average time lapse in the appeals process has fallen from 189 days to below 30 days (Figure 5.1), and federal funding is safe. And the new system and strategy it enables has reduced the state's time to handle unemployment claims by 700 percent.

Figure 5.1 Average Time Lapse in Unemployment Appeals Process, Before and After Implementation

At Bluewolf we considered the department's unemployment claimants as customers and designed the systems to handle claims as we would any customer deserving of prompt, attentive service. The principles we used are the same ones we apply to our own customers: clean, accurate data; timely processing; reduction in backlogs; and attentive service. It pays off.

CUSTOMER ENGAGEMENT

Here at Bluewolf, we go a few steps further with customers than most. More than just attentive service, we are obsessive about the customer experience. For us, customer obsession is about how you organize your resources and build your culture around the customer, and how your resources in turn organize their efforts around the customer. Customer engagement is how you create and deliver the best customer experience without question. Name the top five companies in your opinion for customer engagement and experience, right now. Chances are, at least three of the following made your list:

- Amazon
- Google
- Apple

- Disney
- Xbox (Microsoft)

There is a reason these companies land at the top of the heap every time customer engagement comes up, and it's not because they are the best or biggest companies in the world, although they certainly are leaders in their respective market segment. Walmart dominates the retail market and Exxon/Mobil rules the oil and gas industry, but they aren't even close to making this list. Companies like the five listed have a large, loyal customer base because their primary concerns are the customer journey and the experience their customers have every step of the way. People trust and rely on Google to such an extent that the entire Internet seems to implode if its search engine is down for two minutes. As we know, this doesn't happen often, and the fact that it's fixed in such a minuscule amount of time is impressive, which only serves to increase customer engagement because we all know they can be relied upon.

We take customer attention more seriously than most organizations, but others are recognizing the value of true customer obsession and are trying to do the same. Let's take a moment to explain what we mean by customer obsession. Customer obsession and customer engagement are central tenets of the customer-driven enterprise. It goes far beyond the idiotic clichés about the customer being always right or the customer being number one. In an agile enterprise, the customer is everything all the time. This chapter explains how to become truly customer obsessed, why you want to, and why it is so critical for success in today's economy.

If you haven't realized it yet, the old ways of competing don't apply. The battle for customers is won based on your ability to engage customers completely. That's why we aren't shy about customer obsession.

Have you ever really thought through the incredible customer moments that occur each time you walk into an Apple Store?

Almost the moment you enter, you are greeted by an employee who is not only equipped to answer any question you have about Apple's products, but can check you out on the spot using the iPad they're carrying. No lines, no paper receipts—just a direct, one-on-one interaction that is simple, fluid, and quick. That's a customer-obsessed, agile company that knows how to engage the customer fully, and Apple is extremely successful by almost any measure. (Historical note: When the late Steve Jobs announced his intentions to open retail stores in 2001, his announcement was met with tepid enthusiasm. Today, Apple Stores generate $16 billion annually and boast the highest revenue per square foot of any retailer.) But unfortunately, customer engagement isn't easy. Companies fumble opportunities to engage customers every day.

A leading telecom player, for instance, seems prone to blowing it lately from a customer standpoint. They keep popping up in the news, and not in ways that show them in the best light. For example: A customer's home was lost to a fire, and the provider delayed canceling his subscription (due to the customer's inability to provide his account number) until considerable media exposure and pressure. Rather than having a customer engagement mentality in place that would have enabled them to handle this smoothly, they stumbled when they encountered an extreme situation where they needed to put the customer first.

It could have been so easy to do right by the customer to preserve and even advance the relationship (remember the lifetime value of a customer). Basic employee training on tone, approach, and the handling of unique requests could have prevented this and other similar situations, especially those where employees exhibit customer-inappropriate behavior.

Or maybe you heard the story of the athletic clothing retailer, where the company chairman commented that some women's bodies don't work for their clothing. While the chairman may have been expressing his honest opinion, it was neither sensitive nor appropriate. Following this incident, the company also banned customers who had sold their merchandise on eBay from buying products online by blacklisting their IP addresses. Apparently, it took numerous news stories and customer complaints in the very public forum of Facebook to get them to change their policies. Rather than trying to connect with all of their customers, the company alienated many of them, including the women they thought their clothing suited.

Now, contrast this to the eastern state described previously. They listened to their customers' complaints and noticed the backlogs and delays. Granted, this department had to be threatened with a delay in their reimbursements, but they did the right thing by their customers and never ended up as the lead item in a Facebook timeline or on the front page of *The New York Times.*

Still, the reality is that most businesses are not fully customer focused. This is bad for customers, but it can be good for business managers like you who understand the importance of customer focus and are ready to do something about it. Besides, it makes more competitive sense than trying to match suicidal low prices.

Actually, most businesses subscribe to all the correct clichés like "the customer is always right" or "the customer comes first," never bothering to check what customers want, need, or even what they think. These managers have a product or service *they* think is good and provides value, therefore it must be true. They never hold themselves to a customer experience litmus test, and they don't want to know because then they might have to change their thinking, take remedial actions, or spend money.

CUSTOMER EXPERIENCE 101

The problem: Customer experience is complicated, multidimensional, and you're not the boss. The customers control the relationship, not you. The funnel algorithm that has served the business for so long (Figure 5.2) is no longer enough.

Figure 5.2 Traditional Sales Funnel

Customer experience is the sum of all experiences a consumer has with a supplier of goods or services over the duration of the relationship with that supplier. Today, you're responsible for the experience people have with your brand before they even become a customer and for as long as they remain a customer. Again, think about how much of the lifetime value of the customer you want.

That means thinking of customers as actual people, not transactions; as people whose decisions are based largely on emotional factors and, as far as you're concerned, on their experience with your brand. Simply providing a 360-degree view of your customer won't help you understand them as people. That's the old way—and it never really worked, anyway.

The new way is to build an understanding of the customer on a data foundation and then use that data to feed your employees with predictive customer moments. These would prescribe their next best action based on truly using predictive models to drive customer engagement.

The best way to determine what data needs to be captured is to use customer journey mapping. You have to understand not just the customer life cycle (Figure 5.3) but also map out each and every touch point a customer has with your business. This will enable you to assess your strengths and weaknesses around the

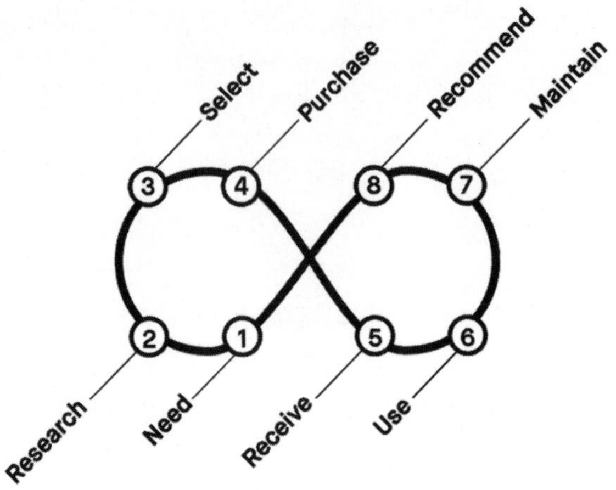

Figure 5.3 The Customer Life Cycle

customer connection. Customer journey and experience mapping consists of seven steps:

1. Select a specific customer to map.
2. Identify the high-level customer life cycle phases.
3. Map the step-by-step customer journey.
4. Map customer touch points.
5. Add customer attitudes and emotions.
6. Define internal supporting structure.
7. Identify opportunities.

Once you have created a visualization of that journey, you'll be able to design solutions that are targeted at improving specific moments to achieve better outcomes.

HOW CUSTOMERS BUY

Do you ever wish customers could simply be cogs in your consumption machine? You could push a button and they would buy over and over again. Unfortunately, they are not cogs in your consumption machine or anyone else's. They are people with thoughts and feelings, trying to balance rational and emotional actions. Despite weighing the pros and cons, conducting research, making checklists, and following all the dutiful buying behaviors, most decisions are made based on emotional factors, which are influenced by their experience with a brand.[1]

In a paper titled "Emotion and Decision Making," researchers Lerner, Li, Valdesolo, and Kassam observe that a revolution in the science of emotion has emerged in the last few decades, bringing about the potential for a paradigm shift in decision theories. The research reveals that emotions constitute powerful, pervasive, and predictable drivers of decision making.[2]

Across different domains, important regularities appear in the mechanisms through which emotions influence judgments and choices. In the resulting paper, the researchers propose an integrated model of decision making that accounts for both traditional (rational-choice theory) inputs and emotional inputs, synthesizing scientific findings to date. In short, they write that in order to have anything like a complete theory of human rationality, we have to understand what role emotion plays in it. Today, we now recognize the crucial role contemporary science has begun to give emotion in decision research. Across disciplines ranging from philosophy to neuroscience, an increasingly vibrant quest to identify the effects of emotion on judgment and decision making is in progress.

Writing in *Psychology Today* in February 2013, Peter Noel Murray reported that emotion is a necessary ingredient to almost all decisions.[3] When we are confronted with a decision, emotions from previous, related experiences affix values to the options we are considering. These emotions create preferences, which lead to our decision. As a result, emotions are the primary reason why consumers prefer brand name products. Why else, he asks, would we pay more for brand name products when many of the products we buy are available as generic brands with the same ingredients and at cheaper prices?

Recent research shows that positive emotions toward a brand have far greater influence on consumer loyalty than trust and other judgments. As a result, consumers are taking their biggest cues from a brand's attributes as they experienced them. And this is why customer obsession and insistence on creating an outstanding brand experience for each customer are so important.

CHANGING THE HISTORICAL MIND-SET

If you want your customers or prospects to do something different—like adopt you as a new provider—you have to change their historical mind-set. This is another way of saying get them to stop doing what they usually do and try something new. That same historical mind-set also stops them from adopting new ideas.

To get them to change, you have to offer an experience that is relevant, fresh, and better than what they have experienced previously. You identify what this experience might be by looking through the data you have been collecting about your customer and learning about their needs, expectations, and hopes. You don't even have to figure it out; if you just pay attention to the data you are collecting, the customers themselves will reveal what they would respond to.

Let's briefly digress to discuss data, because understanding its role will help you know your customer better and deliver better customer experiences, every time. It comes down to achieving a highly predictable, dependable customer experience.

Data science takes every customer interaction and identifies patterns that can be repeated and proactively acted upon. In short, data science enables an organization to get ahead of a customer's actions—to know what customers want even before they do. This powerful ability becomes the focal point for business intelligence and customer engagement strategies, allowing businesses to be more competitive and service oriented as they get closer to their customers than ever before.

The real goal of data science is to integrate the data throughout an organization's business process layer to both predict and provide prescriptive actions to employees who will take the most relevant and timely next step. Yet data science is not confined to empowering just the service and customer-facing employees; it cannot exist in a siloed environment. It must be integrated into the entire organization, prompting businesses to realign executives, employees, and processes around the customer and absorb insight-driven value propositions throughout.

Design and data science must converge to deliver seamless, relevant, and hyper-integrated customer experiences—across channels, devices, and touch points—to reimagine the business and its entire workforce (see Figure 5.4). The result will be a customer-first business, which will bring success going forward.

What you need to do then is to focus on the customer experience from the beginning, and that means operating with a mind-set open to possibilities, not limits. At Bluewolf, we have an exercise we like to call "Art of the Possible." By comparison many, if not most, companies operate according to a

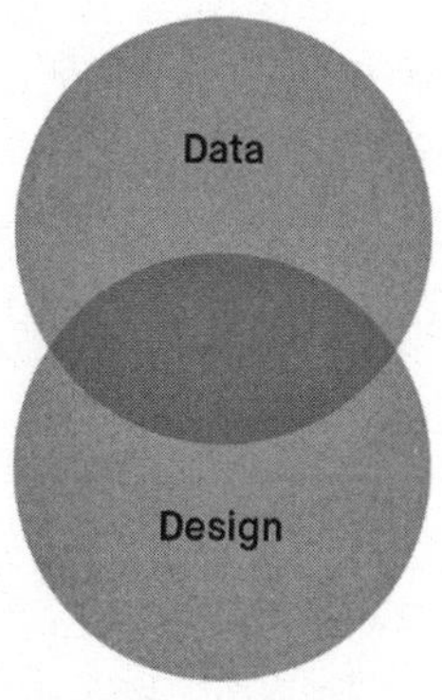

Figure 5.4 Combining Data and Design for Better Results

legacy mind-set. "Art of the Possible" is about moving beyond current practices and embracing new ideas to keep pace with customers and their ever-changing business environment.

Try this little mental exercise: Take your mission statement and replace your company's name with Google. Now, recreate your mission statement while imagining you have all of Google's resources at your fingertips. How does it look when you don't hold back and create a future freely and confidently? Take a step back and analyze how to achieve this reconceived mission, making note of which ideas and attitudes have to change in order to move forward. Often, it's not that companies lack the ability to make a change, but are caught up in old ways of thinking about their business and their customers.

What I'm really asking of you is to challenge yourself to think about the modern customer experience. This is not a one-time, static event you forget about next week. Customer expectations evolve rapidly based on their last, best experience. It's no longer enough to have continuous innovation—you have to provide instantaneous innovation to keep up with the pace of change. When you put customers first and constantly evaluate your business through their eyes, you'll be poised to adapt proactively, not reactively.

Berkshire Hathaway Travel Protection (BHTP)[4] exemplifies this kind of customer-centric thinking center. The company tries to anticipate the needs of its travelers, especially when things have the potential to go wrong. BHTP's AirCare can repair travel mishaps, help locate lost luggage quickly, and even get customers access to the airport lounge. Live service to aid travelers is just a tweet, text, web chat, or call away. With the introduction of AirCare™ in May 2014, BHTP became the first travel-insurance company to address consumers' travel woes by offering a simple, fixed-benefit travel insurance product. It proved the value of a business model that predicts what its customers need, and builds its customer service around those needs.

I have said repeatedly in this book that technology is there to enable solutions, not the solution itself. But to perform this kind of innovation you must have the right tools. In Bluewolf's *The State of Salesforce* report, companies with both cloud governance and application life cycle management (ALM) were three times more likely to attribute revenue growth and two times more likely to attribute improved customer experience to their tool usage.

"Art of the Possible," however, doesn't mean abandoning reality and building castles in the air. It's about being open-minded about realities and customer expectations to optimize them, not succumb to them. Then train yourself and your teams to become customer focused and positioned for success. Constantly ask yourself—where are your customers and opportunities right now, and where do the two meet?

The goal is to move your customers out of their current mindsets. Sometimes this requires some persuasion; in other cases it may involve instantaneous innovation. The idea is to help them leave behind entrenched thinking that won't take them forward and lead them down a better path. To do that, you want to design things that are going to meet the customers' expectations, while knowing full well those expectations will be based on their last best experience. Still, this is not impossible; expectations evolve very rapidly. You can assist by creating experiences that are relevant and up to date. In effect, their last best experience could be the one they just had with you. That's where instantaneous innovation comes into play. You can make outstanding experiences for your customer any time, all the time. And you should.

FEEDING DATA INTO UX DESIGN

Up until this point I have focused on data, but data is only part of the story. Great user experience (UX) design simply represents good data. If you don't know the data, you can't come up with even a passing design, never mind great design. The other thing about great UX design is that it doesn't require anything more of the customer than a normal, intuitive response. Steve Krug laid out the principle of this kind of design in his book *Don't Make Me Think*. Ostensibly about web usability, it really is about ensuring a top customer experience through intuitive design.

Always coming back to the customer, prescriptive design is about creating the use cases around a day in your customers' lives and knowing their journeys. Apply data to feed your design, which should be intuitive. If the action is not immediately obvious, it is not intuitive and therefore contrary to a positive customer experience.

Massive amounts of data, and the accompanying data architecture, have to be organized in such a way that they feed this type of design. Seen in the light of intuition, great design isn't big; it's small and streamlined. This isn't rocket science; to get to great design, step into the shoes of your end users, your customers. Figure out ergonomically what is most feasible in terms of the visual design for the user interface/user experience (UI/UX) and tell the story you've already captured in the data. If you need additional inspiration, Apple offers a wealth of great examples.

The true nature of customer engagement, notes Bluewolf UK's Director Vera Loftis in a December 2015 issue of *Customer Experience*, lies in understanding what customers need before they know they need it—not just resolving cases as they arise.[5] The way you do this is through the combination of analytics, continual monitoring, and collecting customer behavior data. This enables you to predict when a customer is about to have an issue. The tools can alert your people charged with the customer to proactively reach out to a customer before the issue arises, or even communicate directly with the customer. Product or service incidents are inevitable, but going to your customers with a solution before they even know they have a problem is a great way to show them that you care about the issue at hand, and it automatically delivers a superior customer experience even if the initial issue was problematic.

This amounts to what you might call a hyper-integrated customer experience. By contrast, an example of a disconnected experience, Loftis points out, is going into a store and being unable to return an item purchased online because the brand's website is a separate system. This is frustrating, inconvenient, and costly to the customer, which makes it potentially costly to the business, too. Brands need to ensure that they are delivering the same experience across all channels, devices, and touch points. This is what the savvy marketers call an omnichannel experience, where customers experience the same information and service no matter how they choose to do business with the company. With the omnichannel experience, customers can even mix and match communication channels and service people and still experience the same consistent, high-quality service. No matter where the customer is, the experience should be the same. Clean, accurate, consistent data can accomplish this. To understand the customer experience, start by identifying all customer touch points, mapping them to the appropriate data, finding the gaps, and filling them.

Emerging from all of this is the new customer experience. Forget about the 360-degree view. What you really want now is the predictive customer experience view. This isn't about who buys what, when, and where. It's about what's going to happen next. Then you position yourself to take prescriptive action to serve their needs before they're even aware of them. That requires setting up your systems to comb through every detail of available customer data, the data you have been collecting and analyzing to better know your customer. Now, analyze it again using the predictive algorithms that are becoming available, then rinse and repeat.

The road to predictive may seem daunting, but it's more than possible—it's necessary. Let's take a look at the seemingly out-of-the-box ways data and predictive algorithms can improve the customer experience with a discussion of the real-life story told in the best-selling novel *Moneyball*. If you're not familiar with the story, the Oakland Athletics' general manager Billy Beane dramatically improved the A's performance via data analysis. Beane took the on-base percentage data and used it to recruit and sign players who may not have had the most impressive field performance, but were able to get on base, score runs, and win ball games. This had a significant impact on the customer experience, as their higher performance created a better, more exciting game and atmosphere.

Data has the potential to impact everything about your business. Don't you want to figure out the right questions to ask so you can apply the Moneyball scenario and bring success to your own organization?

GET PERSONAL

To paraphrase the messages regularly doled out to parents of teenagers: do you know where your customers are and what they want next? That's the customer challenge I call getting personal. Getting personal means creating a customer experience that is so relevant and appropriate to the customer and the situation that it had to be the result of deep, predictive insight, insight that is so attuned to the customer and the business's needs that it borders on intimate.

The goal of getting personal is to optimize the customer experience, which entails familiarity with a number of customer touch points such as inventory, customer life cycle, and customer experience mapping. And don't just stop with your direct customer. Extend your knowledge to the customer's customer wherever you can. Have you noticed that manufacturers of food products like Doritos advertise heavily to the consumers of those products? Their actual customers—the ones who order the products from the company—are large retailers or distributors. Just look at the extremely costly Super Bowl halftime ads. Costing several million dollars per 30 seconds of air-time, they are targeted to the end users of the products, not the organizations that actually buy the products from the advertiser.

On top of that, these advertisers spend millions of dollars more to research and get to know these end users as much, or more than, they know their actual direct customers. These heavy investments in market research and analysis make sure they are accomplishing the following:

1. Communicating effectively with their target markets,
2. Ensuring that the highly produced and expensive TV spots hit the right notes with the mass Super Bowl audience, and
3. Positioning themselves to deliver the experience these potential customers desire and now expect in terms of style, attitude, performance, and more. In the end, it comes down to establishing a personal relationship between the customer and the brand.

To make this work, establish your data architecture as the single source of truth about your customers: a deep, insightful repository of facts, customer opinions and attitude, sentiment, hopes, expectations, and more; past, present, and (predictive) future. Start with employee checkups and customer check-ins, but don't stop there. And please, don't send generic, bland surveys—they don't work.

Instead, put yourself into your employees' shoes—understand their daily journey and, in turn, how that affects the customer journey. If you never have, try Rep Rides, Bluewolf's day-in-the-life workshop explained in detail in Chapter 10. Here's an example where Rep Rides made a difference:

Bay Club

The Bay Club, an active lifestyle and hospitality company with a network of 24 modern country clubs across 10 campuses in California, did just that. Headquartered in San Francisco, the growing enterprise serves 85,000 members and is home to 3,400 associates. However, the company wanted to become more than just a fitness brand. Its goal was to become a family lifestyle company—a modern-day country club catering to affluent households. The executives planned to use a data-driven approach to learn about their customers' needs and wants. They also wanted better reporting capabilities that integrated data from multiple sources to generate a holistic view of their pipeline and business.

PROBLEM

The company already was a Salesforce user, but they weren't maximizing its value. They were using multiple systems across sales and marketing to manage customer relationships and lacked system standards, leading to data quality issues and lost productivity. Have you heard this before here? It's a pretty common problem we encounter all the time. In order to meet aggressive growth goals, including increased cross-selling and higher membership retention rates, The Bay Club needed a partner to help them expand use, generate new ideas, and redefine their processes to support scale in the business.

SOLUTION

The Bluewolf team first set out to tackle the company's customer data issues and immediately encountered a lack of system governance. The managers at each club would enter data differently. What should be the correct way? Good question. In order to accurately determine the optimal process, the team initiated our Rep Rides methodology to identify critical system gaps and inefficiencies, and to identify a new, ideal sales process.

Through Rep Rides, the team identified efficiency gaps in employee workflows, prescribed and built solutions that streamlined data collection and integration, and then rolled out a change management plan to ensure employees understood the new system and processes. They also advised a hybrid cloud approach that integrated data into Salesforce from online surveys, retail and spa purchases, net promoter scores, and member forums to get an accurate picture of who their customers are and their buying patterns.

RESULTS

With this help, Bay Club executives now have the data and pipeline view needed to make effective management decisions. They can now find the right prospects, maximize a complex sales process, and increase their customer close rates. Management also doubled the number of clubs in less than six months.

ART OF THE POSSIBLE

Can you do the same? Sure. Start by challenging your company to think beyond what is available, to what just might be possible. Strip outmoded mind-sets. Then engage with customer mind-sets toward business processes. That means capturing the current experience based on their last best experience. Then start innovating.

Finally, build on the customer experience, which is intimately tied to employee engagement—don't bother trying to optimize one without the other. And of course, make it personal and consistent. Remember, look through their eyes, not yours. Then expand on your strategy of information, understanding, empathy, and action. Sounds simple, huh?

People complain that I make it sound too simple, that I have drunk too deeply from the Kool-Aid of customer obsession. Needless to say, I don't agree. Just read through this book and try just one or two of the things I suggest. Then reach out to me at Bluewolf's headquarters in New York and give me your honest opinion.

6

How to Win the Talent War

Picture this: A major financial services organization has an information technology (IT) staff of 1,500 across multiple locations. While management wants to reduce costs and boost performance, there is dissatisfaction in the ranks. This scenario is so typical that it could apply to half the readers of this book, maybe more. This particular company's previous attempts at transformation didn't work, leaving its employees disengaged and cynical about the future.

Management still had high hopes. Through process transformation, it revamped all project management and IT processes, leading to efficient and consistent ways of working, which led to confident and predictable IT service delivery. Management also wanted to initiate a high-performance culture while raising the bar on expected skills and behaviors, especially increasing IT professionalism and knowledge sharing. Finally, it hoped to build engagement in its transformation program.

With the help of consultants, management settled on a strategy to create specialized communities of practice within IT. It brought in key stakeholders and identified the areas of high potential as communities of practice targets. The idea was to deliver business benefit as soon as possible. These communities of practice would then be integrated with the business's usual processes.

Right off the bat, management realized it had to identify and engage the right people fast to lead the practice communities. It knew many were already in demand elsewhere. It also needed to secure initial buy-in and support. Once up and running, it wanted to keep the community agenda manageable and business-focused. Finally, management insisted on the inclusion of all employees into at least one community.

This was at least the company's second pass at revamping its IT workforce, and it didn't want to replay previous failure. Fortunately, this time it achieved results it was happy with. Specifically, it

- Replaced inefficient processes and earned external accreditation
- Improved throughput of service delivery
- Significantly increased knowledge sharing between IT professionals and the various teams
- Experienced a 10 percentage-point improvement in levels of employee engagement and satisfaction
- Improved recruitment and rebalancing of permanent-to-contractor roles
- Achieved strategic workforce development and proactive management of talent
- Enabled transformational change

This company's experience leads me to wonder why its previous efforts at workforce transformation failed. I'd also like to know how it is doing since these initial results were reported. Their experience shows how difficult it is to gather and organize a collection of individuals to perform the mission of the organization. Getting it right is not a sure thing. Remember, you're dealing with people here. As I noted previously, workers have lives outside of work; lives that impact their performance for better or worse.

Many industry pundits contend that data is the most valuable asset and one that is continuously growing by the hour. I'm a huge believer in the value of data; we rely on it all the time. Still, talent—the people you hire to staff your operation—is by far the most valuable asset a customer-obsessed business can have. And unlike data, it is not an asset that is continually growing. To the contrary, there is a global competition for the best talent, a competition companies like yours probably want to win. Customer-focused companies have an insatiable craving for the very best talent they can find and then become maniacal in leveraging that talent through social collaboration.

Talent is an all-encompassing term for your ideal employee—technically, culturally, in every way that is important to your team and to your customers. You will have to pin down what the term *talent* means for your organization—the textbook definition from human resources probably won't suffice for a dynamic, customer-driven organization. Better to work with your recruiting team, those who are actively engaged in finding and attracting talent, to understand specifically what that means for your company. While the term *talent* is intentionally general, your application of it needs to be specific to your needs, culture, and values.

Everybody has an opinion on talent. Let's get the caveats and disclaimers out right up front. Everybody may be created equal in principle, but that is not the case when you are looking for talent to staff your operation. You need people who not only bring the specific skills to do the job, but the outlook to mesh with and contribute to your organization. This will not be just anybody.

Similarly, there is a difference between a gifted employee and an engaged employee. No matter how gifted an employee may be, if he or she is not engaged in what your organization is doing and how it works, the value of that employee's gifts will be reduced. In short, don't settle for skill sets at the expense of a cultural fit. In the previous chapter, you read about the dangers and costs of a disengaged employee. In this chapter, you'll learn why you want to seek employees who will be engaged or, at the very least, who are gifted and can become actively engaged.

Don't just look for really smart people, the high IQ and extremely high IQ folks. Sure, it makes for exciting TV shows like *Scorpion*, but it doesn't always translate well to the office. Instead, aim to hire for high emotional intelligence. People with high emotional intelligence make better team players, managers, and leaders. According to research conducted by Annie McKee on behalf of *Harvard Business Review*, they are better able to deal with stress, overcome obstacles, and inspire others to work toward collective goals. In the same way, people with high emotional intelligence manage conflict with less fallout and build stronger teams.[1] Finally, they are generally happier at work.

What McKee describes as emotional intelligence can also be seen as basic good social skills and manners. This was the kind of stuff we all should have learned from our mothers as they shipped us off to kindergarten. Does anyone still remember a book that came out over 30 years ago—*All I Really Need to Know I Learned in Kindergarten* by Robert Fulghum? It's actually still available on Amazon; apparently its lessons have withstood the test of time.

However, many managers, McKee observed, lack even basic self-awareness and social skills. (They obviously didn't pay attention in kindergarten.) As a result, they don't recognize the impact of their own feelings and moods. How then are they supposed to adapt to the demands of today's fast-paced world? Even worse, they don't demonstrate basic empathy for others. As a result, they don't understand people's needs, which means they are unable to meet those needs or inspire people to act. Does that sound like any managers you've ever worked for?

You may think that some positions, usually technical in nature, don't really require emotional intelligence. Yet every position to some extent is social. Most employees are not trapped in their cubicles; usually, they are part of a team and are expected to attend meetings. All of this involves collaboration, conflict resolution, compromise, and similar social skills. If you are aspiring to become a customer-focused organization, you want people with higher emotional intelligence. Finding them can be tricky. It requires sufficient emotional intelligence on your part and then guiding personal interviews that can make these capabilities apparent.

Up to this point, this chapter has focused on what a customer-focused organization wants in terms of talent. That's only half the equation. The other half entails what people want most from a good job. A good job, as Gallup defines it, is one that gives a person the amount of work he or she needs, but also defines their relationship with their community, their city, their country, and their whole world as they understand it. That definition, however, was researched and written over 10 years ago and the results published five years ago. A good job now has to include so much more: work-life balance, giving back, the ability to make a difference, and the list goes on.

A 2015 report on millennials from the U.S. Chamber of Commerce found that three out of four millennials reported that work-life balance drives their career choices.[2] And many companies are indeed starting to offer flexible work schedules, work-from-home policies, and job appraisals based on outcomes and deliverables.

However, in an article published in the *Harvard Business Review* in February 2016, author Tracy Benson found that even flexibility may not be enough to motivate and retain millennials.[3] Businesses will have to go further to keep these workers truly engaged, she continued, starting with adapting management and communication styles to engage millennials and improve productivity and outcomes across the board.

As it turns out, it is rare to find millennials who intend to spend their entire career with one company. Chalk this up to the changes between the career-oriented workers of the past and the self-identified millennial change agents of today. Most young workers focus more on what they can achieve for themselves—and, as important, for the world around them—than on building a corporate career. Clearly, these are not the self-centered, self-absorbed, selfish young people as some have characterized them. They like to take risks and make bold moves forward, and just as important, they care about their community. But whether you agree with them or not, they are the key to winning the crucial coming jobs war, according to Gallup. How key? Eighty million plus, the largest census cohort size in history, and bigger by far than the baby boomers, whom marketers spent decades wooing.

Meeting millennials' interests in socially relevant work is not difficult. verynice, a Los Angeles-based design agency, engages in 50 percent for profit and 50 percent pro bono work, a business model that its founder, Matt Manos, developed as a senior at UCLA. It's about more than donating money. verynice asks a challenging question, which is a very millennial thing from the start: Which is worth more—donating \$100 to charity or five hours of your expertise (which took years of effort and training) to help them build something better? Of course, not all companies can make such an effort sustainable, but the verynice model for giving back has huge potential. Another model to admire is Salesforce's Pledge 1% initiative, of which Bluewolf is a member. These types of programs are about supporting a stronger community and serving beyond yourself, an idea that resonates strongly with today's incoming workforce.

As a member of Pledge 1%, Bluewolf has an internal initiative called "Pack Gives Back" (as in Bluewolf Pack—our employees—give back) to support those types of efforts. In response to the growing talent gap of technical skills training in local communities, Bluewolf has committed to dedicating 1 percent of our resources to educate, empower, and enable youth through digital literacy guidance, personal and professional development, and mentorship. To drive the message further, we encourage employees to contribute 20 volunteer hours per year toward Bluewolf-sponsored activities. Of course, we've added a gamification twist to spur employees to contribute more of their time; Bluewolf will award a matching grant to those who have contributed the most time to their chosen nonprofit, and billable employees can earn utilization hours for their time spent volunteering.

Before we started this program, many of our employees were already volunteering. Pack Gives Back is a way for us to amplify their individual efforts and make an even bigger impact on our community.

ATTRITION: CURSE OR BLESSING

Sometimes attrition can be a blessing, such as when an employee you didn't want decides to leave, hopefully giving you ample notice. More often, attrition can be a curse, as when carefully cultivated employees leave for someplace else. Either way, attrition costs you. It is expensive to find, onboard, and train employees and nurture them to the point where they are fully productive.

Attrition is also inevitable. Some managers mistakenly think they can prevent attrition by blocking contact with headhunters, thereby stopping them from raiding their best employees. They don't realize that anybody worth hiring already has their résumé posted on LinkedIn and other social sites. If you really want to fend off the headhunters, run a great operation that truly engages its workers. It's not all about money; it's about engaging your employees and being responsive to them.

If you need confirmation, a Gallup study released in 2015 found that about 50 percent of the 7,200 adults surveyed left a job to escape their manager (Figure 6.1). In other words, they were driven away not because they were underpaid or not promoted, but because they had a bad manager.

So what do bad managers do or not do to drive away employees? They fail to communicate with their workers personally, sincerely, and substantively, and not just about target goals or revenue targets. In short, workers want real communication.

The researchers found that workers whose managers hold regular meetings are three times more likely to be engaged—that is, feel involved in and enthusiastic about their jobs. Workers said they want to be in contact with bosses on a daily basis, and not just about sales targets or an upcoming presentation. They want their manager to take an interest in their personal lives, too.

In fact, just over half of the survey respondents gave the highest agreement rating to the statement: "I feel I can approach my manager with any type of question." These are the workers who are actively engaged. By comparison, roughly a quarter of respondents said they did not feel comfortable bringing up

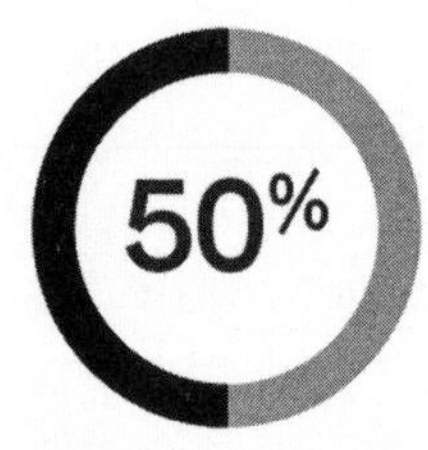

Figure 6.1 Gallup's "State of the American Manager"

personal matters with their managers. They may otherwise be model employees, but somehow they feel a barrier between themselves and the company.

Jim Harter, chief scientist for Gallup's workplace and well-being research, wrote in *The Wall Street Journal*, "Employees who feel they can communicate openly tend to place deep trust in their bosses. . . . [Those workers have] an element of certainty in the [supervisor-subordinate] relationship that's really powerful."[4]

Setting job priorities and goals is another area plagued by problems, but with huge potential for improvement. Workers who feel like they're given little guidance or understanding about what's expected of them are uncomfortable. Just remember the lessons of the employee culture; your employees want certainty, and clear expectations have to be a part of that. In the Gallup survey, 12 percent of workers strongly agreed that their manager helps set work priorities, and those workers tended to be much happier than those who scored their bosses' goal-setting at the bottom end of the scale (Figure 6.2). Clarity of expectations is perhaps the most basic of employee needs and is vital to performance.

Accountability, or rather the lack of it, is another area that bothers workers. "For engaged employees, accountability means that all employees are held to roughly to the same standards, and

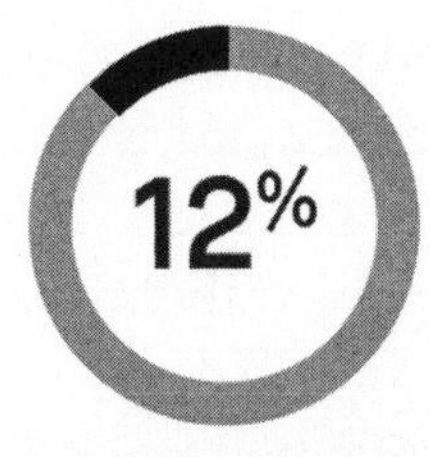

Figure 6.2 Gallup's "State of the American Manager"

slackers will be exposed," said Harter. That level of accountability translates into equity.

Remember, the employee culture has been conditioned by generations of bad managers to be cynical and skeptical of management. Deep down, however, the culture does want to trust managers and have an element of certainty. In effect, the employee culture needs that trust and certainty if it is ever to become truly engaged, which is what every manager should want, too. Trustworthy management, especially in the form of trustworthy direct managers, can go a long way toward increasing retention. But it only takes one mistake to violate that trust, which should be regarded as a very fragile yet extremely valuable commodity—hard to earn and easily lost.

So how do you satisfy your employees' need for communication and support, and increase retention? At Bluewolf, we've developed a standard program series to do just that: Ascend (onboarding), Management Academy, and Dashboards (measurement/accountability).

ASCEND

Improving retention starts the day the employee arrives with a thorough, positive onboarding experience. At Bluewolf, we start by acclimating our new hires to our culture and fill them in on everything they will need to know about us from a community and resource perspective. Ascend is our formalized onboarding process, which is run by our Global Talent Management Team. Other teams that help in onboarding at Bluewolf are our recruitment team, HR, and IT.

You can be assured that when you start work at Bluewolf you will never be lonely, at least not in the first couple of months. God help you if you just want a quiet lunch alone. There will be scheduled meetings with your manager, your assigned mentor, and your team itself, and maybe a separate meeting with your team leader. In addition, IT will meet with you to set up your systems, and HR will want to connect with you to ease you through all the paperwork. Sadly, we have yet to find any way to completely eliminate all the bureaucracy. At those meetings and any other encounters, scheduled or casual, people will ask you how you're doing, whether you need anything, and how they might be able to help you.

MANAGEMENT ACADEMY

I've talked quite a bit about the need for managers to communicate with employees and set a regular cadence of goal setting and review. But being a manager is about more than checking off boxes on an employee satisfaction chart; it's about leadership, and it's about empathy. To help our managers develop and improve those qualities, we offer a series of programs and resources. The first offering is Elevate, a three-day management workshop held twice annually. Broken down into three sections (managing me, managing others, managing the business), the workshop has our managers role-play difficult scenarios, refine communication techniques and strategies, and learn how to align their teams with Bluewolf's larger strategic goals. To support these workshops throughout the year, we host virtual Manager Moment sessions to help address any problems managers run into, and we also have a Manager Moments app, a custom app to access tips, tools, and resources from a mobile phone or tablet.

Remember, it's in your best interest to empower your managers with the tools they need to lead their teams effectively. Take the time to figure out what your employees need to manage better, and then put it into practice. In turn, their direct reports will feel better heard and more in control of their future with the company, leading them to want to *stay* with the company.

DASHBOARDS

When trying to improve both talent acquisition *and* employee retention, data is your best friend. When you are losing employees, which departments are bleeding the most, and which are the healthiest? Are you experiencing greater attrition rates at particular times of the year? What's the year-over-year average? What's the gender ratio?

If you don't have access to this data, you won't be able to improve retention, plain and simple. Bluewolf has a standard retention dashboard that is updated daily so that we can see improvements, challenges, and problem areas in real time (see Figure 6.3). While our HR and Global Talent Management teams maintain the dashboard, managers no longer have to rely on them for access to retention metrics when trying to improve the strength of their teams. Everyone is empowered to own their employee-manager relationships, from equal access to data to our mobile resource app.

As a manager, if you communicate with your employees, you will have less attrition, or at least you won't be caught by surprise when somebody leaves. Like customer churn, employees who

Figure 6.3 Example of Employee Metrics Dashboard

depart leave clues that your data collection and analysis should pick up. If you made a point to keep in touch with employees, you could probably pick those preparing to leave in advance of their departure. Of course, there are employees who will have clandestine interviews and drop deceptive signals to disguise their intentions. But if people want to leave, let them go graciously; you don't want to manage your workforce like a police state.

The only exception to your retention efforts might be employees who are actively disengaged, meaning they are deliberately sabotaging the work of their team or relationships with customers. You want to identify them as fast and early as possible and get them out quickly.

For those who leave the company, insist on an exit interview, usually conducted by HR or an outside resource. Keep the data anonymous, but use it to improve your retention and recruiting efforts. Here are the top four questions Bluewolf's HR team uses during exit interviews:

- How well did the job match (or not match) your expectations?
- Did you feel that the work you performed aligned with your personal goals and interests?
- Did you have the tools and resources you needed to effectively do your job?
- Would you recommend this as a (good, fair, enjoyable—substitute your own appropriate adjective) place for a friend to work?

If they reply yes to the last question and you liked the departing employee, ask them to refer any friends if, indeed, you are hiring.

Your HR or legal departments may also have their own ideas, so be sure to check with them. Additionally, the web is full of examples of exit interview questions, so you should never find yourself stuck with nothing worthwhile to ask. And don't forget to actively *record* and *use* this data to improve your retention and recruiting efforts going forward.

AGILE AND ELASTIC

Agile companies need an elastic, flexible, and versatile workforce. *Agile* and *elastic* have almost passed into the buzzword stage and are on track toward becoming cliché. Nonetheless, many organizations continue to adopt elastic and agile concepts as they strive to become more competitive and better able to roll with a rapidly changing business environment.

Among all the things you could make agile or elastic, your workers still represent the most agile variable in the organizational equation. To put it another way, it is easier, faster, and cheaper to reorganize, redeploy, and retrain your people than it is to relocate facilities, retool plants, or change your customers.

One of the strategies agile companies employ is outsourcing (not to be confused with offshoring). At Bluewolf, we see outsourcing as a community of highly skilled freelancers that ebb and flow with the needs of the company. Rather than a passing fad or a last-ditch cost-cutting strategy of a financially stressed company, IT outsourcing has evolved into a strategic tool that reflects our rapidly changing business and technology landscape. While once used as a tourniquet to stem bleeding resources, it has matured and become a strategic tool for fast-moving businesses and industries.

In another drive to agility, companies need to explore partnerships. It is clear the business environment has grown so complex and competitive that no company can meet every customer need alone. Customer-focused companies need to be prepared to engage partners to deliver capabilities they can't deliver on their own (or risk losing the customer). Bluewolf partners with a small handful of companies, preferring to maintain and enhance our core capabilities in-house. However, there are some instances where Bluewolf customers may need specialized applications, and our partnerships with companies like Apttus and InsideSales help us deliver complete solutions.

Between a thorough effort to cultivate and hire the right talent for your organization, and successfully onboarding and retaining that talent, you have most of the recruitment bases covered. Take pains to avoid the "jack-of-all-trades and master-of-none" approach, which is both costly and ineffective. When you need to fill the inevitable talent gaps—often the result of emerging opportunities or changing customer expectations—you can fill them through part-time contractors, outsourcing, or selective partnerships. If you are committed to being a customer-focused organization, you now have a number of ways to find and deliver the capabilities and service your customers demand.

WORK-LIFE BALANCE

In the not too distant past, work-life balance never came up as an issue in corporate life. The exception was when some critical star personally made it an issue. Management would grudgingly make the minimal accommodations to keep this employee on board, at least until the company felt safe enough to dispense with their particular talent altogether.

More recently, that thinking has changed. An increasingly large number of managers recognize that work-life balance is a key component of an organization's success. In the global war for talent, it isn't always easy to replace a productive worker. The worker, in fact, may not even be a star performer. In a well-managed organization, every employee has a role to play, and replacing any employee entails both expense and risk. The challenge becomes how best to set up a workforce so that everyone's personal situation (within reason) can be accommodated. Most managers now realize that it makes good policy to accommodate their employees' lifestyle needs.

In short, if your strategy requires that you have the best possible talent, you need to be prepared to make sacrifices required to attract and keep that talent. Often, in work-life balance situations the issue may not even be money. It more likely involves schedule flexibility or the need to accommodate a family care situation. It may require IT or HR or even top management to exhibit a level of flexibility to accommodate the particular need.

Some think this is a millennial worker thing, but it is not. Millennials certainly talk about work-life balance, but the issue was floating around before millennials started impacting the workforce. At Bluewolf, we implemented work-life balance policies at the start, long before millennials started arriving here in large numbers.

Complicating work-life balance is the demise of the 9-to-5 workday. In those days, workers showed up at 9 AM, left at 5 PM and the rest of the day was their own. Gone are those easily segmented days that separated work life and personal life. Today, workers feel they must always be available, at least in customer-focused organizations. Opportunities can pop up anytime, anywhere. Similarly, with expanded capabilities of mobile, cloud, and social applications, business expectations around worker availability are changing. Now it's up to you, the worker, to stake your work-life balance priorities and communicate that to management.

Businesses that run in the cloud are more suited to flexible schedules. They can be accessed anywhere, and a chair in an office at a specific location is not required to contribute. Life happens—be aware of it, accept it, own it, and then implement a system that allows you to accommodate a diverse workforce.

TECHNICAL SKILLS

Everybody needs some level of technical skill just to effectively navigate mobile, social, and cloud systems every day. But that's not my concern. My concerns are that every modern business needs outstanding technical talent to support growth in our organizations and the talent war is driving salaries through the roof. If you're not a Fortune 500 company, how can your growing business compete?

The answer: you need to redefine talent. Start by recognizing that you probably don't need graduates from MIT to create a tech powerhouse in your organization. What you need are people who are technically literate, meaning they are sufficiently familiar with technology to get a substantial benefit from it. They don't have to invent it, troubleshoot it, or build it from scratch. Some of the best employees may be those who don't have the best technical skills but can communicate clearly and facilitate communication between others. These soft skills—active listening, communication, thinking, and critical observation—may be more valuable than star technical skills. People with soft skills contribute to higher levels of employee engagement and can truly inspire great ideas in your organization.

To find them, focus on sourcing candidates who demonstrate these types of qualities and soft skills to support the growth of a strong team. Not all will have the most impressive technical background. Widen your search pool by determining which skills you absolutely need on day one and which can be taught on the job. Don't fight for the shiniest résumé—there are plenty of companies who can and will outbid you. Look instead for individuals who want to work for how much they can give and not how much they can get. That may seem overly idealistic, but my experience suggests it's not.

Start by grooming promising people you already have. Yeah, I know the complaint: if we train them, they will just leave for a higher-paying job. My response: pay people a competitive wage—not necessarily the highest in your market, but a competitive one. People will appreciate that you invested in them and pay you back by being more productive and adding to your skills inventory. Besides, grooming people to succeed is the right thing to do, not just for the company but for them.

At Bluewolf, we actually tap our own employees to teach their skills to other employees in the areas of project management, technical competencies (mobile, Application Lifecycle Management [ALM], analytics), Salesforce certifications, and soft skills (conflict resolution, conducting productive meetings, and so on). Employees who teach skills win points in our gamification program to qualify for some big prizes. We also support continuing education with tuition reimbursement. If you can't underwrite tuition, other options include arranging online talks, setting up seminars and lectures, or anything else that will provide opportunities to expose your people to skills that will build the company. None of this has to be expensive. You can always find local college instructors who will teach for what amounts to a modest honorarium.

So where do you find the talent you need, especially if you aren't going to cultivate it internally or pay big dollars to recruiters? I'm tempted to say wherever you can, but I can do better than that. Here are some recruiting options:

- On-campus recruiting; don't forget community colleges
- Trade schools
- Partnerships with career shift training programs like General Assembly
- Coop programs, which will lead you back to colleges
- Programs that help working moms reenter the workforce. They have tons of experience but often encounter little opportunity when trying to get a job after a few years off. Be

prepared to be flexible; moms returning to the workforce most likely will have a child or a few who still need periodic attention. In addition to their experience from their pre-mom life, however, they probably have a lot of social and collaborative skills honed from serving on endless committees at the PTA, their church, or myriad community groups. And they probably have patience, which you may also need, at least at first.

- Military veterans—they bring a wide array of skills, experience, discipline, and a desire to work.

CONCLUSION: DRASTICALLY COMPETITIVE JOB MARKET

The big competition is for whatever talent you need. It's not about some particular job you are looking to fill. Anyway, jobs are not what they used to be and candidates are expecting more and more from the companies they come to work for. It's not necessarily about high salaries, big benefits, or nifty perks—ping-pong tables, beer in the fridge, pizza Fridays. It's really about personal and professional fulfillment and satisfaction. As you work on defining and improving your company culture, benefits, and employee focus, don't just focus on attracting new talent, although that is critical. Also focus on keeping the employees you already have by providing them with a better experience, too. In the end, a rich company culture can go far in compensating for a less competitive salary. Understand how to define your culture and then market your brand to potential employees to find the best fit, for both of you. Focus on your culture, creative hiring practices, flexibility, partnerships, and professional development to solve your resource problems and attract and retain the talent that will be essential for helping you serve your customers and achieve success.

Let's give Jim Clifton, the Gallup CEO and author of *The Coming Job Wars*, the last word on jobs and hiring: "The biggest problem facing the world is an inadequate supply of good jobs. . . . Job creation is the new currency of all world leaders. The new most important social value in the world no longer relates to human rights, the environment, abortion, religion, gay marriage, women's issues, or equality. The number one social value in the world is the next position you are trying to fill."[5] We take it seriously at Bluewolf; hopefully you take it seriously, too.

7

Gender Diversity Isn't a Plus, It's a Business Imperative

When I was attending my daughter's varsity basketball game last spring, I took a few minutes to observe the crowd around me in the bleachers and noticed something interesting. Many of the women in attendance were sitting toward the top of the bleachers, grouped together closely to both enjoy the game and socialize, while the men watching the game were spaced a few feet apart along the benches. They bantered back and forth, exchanged fist bumps and high fives after good plays, but their social interactions were otherwise limited.

I'm not here to advance a theory about the reasons why those men and women behaved differently at the basketball game, but it did raise a few questions about the social habits and personality traits of men and women. There is no doubt that, when observed as a group, men and women tend to behave differently from one another. Whether those differences are a result of the social and cultural expectations of the times or are due to other factors is a difficult question to answer, but the fact remains that observable differences in behavior do exist.

That very point, that differences exist, that they are palpable, demonstrable, and have far-reaching impact, is the starting point for this discussion of why gender diversity matters. Nature promotes diversity all the time, even if that isn't always reflected in our culture at large. Take, for example, a 1995 study where Swiss scientist Claus Wedekind had women smell the undershirts worn by seven different men and rank them according to their level of attraction. Upon analysis, each woman was most attracted to the shirt worn by the man whose immune system differed from hers the most.[1] In other words, genetic diversity was the better choice.

The question is, if we agree that diversity is a good thing, why don't we see more of it? This chapter examines the current gender diversity climate in the business world and will make a case for its social and economic importance. In my mind, there is no question: achieving gender diversity is a must for any company that wants to remain competitive and grow their business.

STATE OF DIVERSITY TODAY

Gender diversity in the tech and business worlds seems to operate along the same dynamics as media and television (70/30, and depending on how you measure it, tech is even worse). It seems to me that companies may be in need of a business-oriented Bechdel test. For those of you unfamiliar with it, the Bechdel test is a criteria-based yardstick used to measure the levels of gender diversity and female representation in the media. To pass the Bechdel test, a program must satisfy the following requirements:

1. The program has to have at least two women in it,
2. who talk to each other,
3. about something besides a man.

It seems simple enough, right? But you'd be surprised to learn that in a survey of over 1,600 films from 1970–2013, only 53 percent passed the test. In 47 percent of those films, there wasn't a single scene that satisfied those simple rules. You'd never find those rates of failure if the test focused on men. As one critic sardonically put it, "Plots need to advance, after all."[2]

But here's the really interesting thing: movies that pass the Bechdel test, that give female characters more substantial roles, earn higher returns relative to those that fail. In a 2014 study, FiveThirtyEight found that "the films that passed the test had about a 37 percent higher return on investment (ROI) in the United States, and the same ROI internationally, compared to films that did not pass the test."[3] Overall, gender diversity leads to greater financial gain in the film industry and, as you'll see, has the potential for similar impact in business.

What would a business Bechdel test look like? My criteria would be a bit stricter than those applied to media:

1. A business would need to hit a minimum ratio of 45/55 of men and women in either direction,
2. where at least two women are included on every project,
3. and who represent half of C-suite leadership.

I'll be the first to admit that Bluewolf currently does not satisfy each of these requirements, but we are working on it. We are closest to satisfying the project rule and currently have at least two women working on 72 percent of our projects. Three out of nine members of our executive leadership team are women—Corinne Sklar, CMO; Jolene Chan, chief of staff; and Caryn Fried, VP global talent management—and our current workforce ratio is 35 percent women to 65 percent men (see Figures 7.1 and 7.2). As I said, we have work to do, but we are committed to change, not just in the name of equality but because it makes good business sense.

Figure 7.1 Bluewolf Executive Staff Gender Breakdown

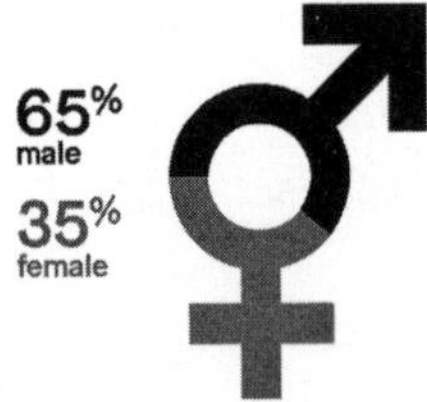

Figure 7.2 Bluewolf Gender Ratio

ECONOMIC CASE FOR GENDER DIVERSITY

There are many social crusaders who pursue gender equality and diversity solely on the strength of moral righteousness. I am not one of those people. It's not that I disbelieve or don't support the inherent social good of the movement, but I find a stronger case can be made when looking at these issues from an economic standpoint. And as we know, a rising tide lifts all boats.

Let's begin with a discussion about education. According to the Center for American Progress, women:

- Earn almost 60 percent of undergraduate degrees and 60 percent of all master's degrees;
- Earn 47 percent of all law degrees and 48 percent of all medical degrees;

- Earn more than 44 percent of master's degrees in business and management, including 37 percent of MBAs; and
- Make up 47 percent of the U.S. labor force and 59 percent of the college-educated, entry-level workforce.[4]

And yet, women:

- Are only 14.6 percent of executive officers, 8.1 percent of top earners, and 4.6 percent of Fortune 500 CEOs;
- Hold just 16.9 percent of Fortune 500 board seats;
- Make up 54.2 percent of the labor force in the financial services industry, but are only 12.4 percent of executive officers and 18.3 percent of board directors. None are CEOs;
- Account for 78.4 percent of the labor force in health care and social assistance but only 14.6 percent of executive officers and 12.4 percent of board directors. None, again, are CEOs; and
- Hold only 9 percent of management positions in information technology and account for only 14 percent of senior management positions at Silicon Valley startups.[5]

Women make up nearly half of the workforce and hiring pool. They are earning more undergraduate and graduate degrees than men, and some studies indicate the trend will continue to increase. If you want the most skilled and talented workforce, you need to hire and retain women as well as men. If you don't make it a priority to expand your search pool, you'll be missing out on a highly skilled, motivated workforce.

According to Judith Warner, author of the Center for American Progress report, at the current rate of change, "it will take until 2085 for women to reach parity with men in leadership roles in our country." In my mind, to accept that standard is to accept failure. At our current speed of innovation, we can't afford to falter in our pursuit of the economic potential of gender diversity. The rest of the country may choose to move forward at a snail's pace, but those who embrace this challenge and move toward gender parity will reap the benefits at the expense of those who drag their feet.

A McKinsey report released in September 2015 found that if the global population reached its full potential scenario of bridging the gender gap, it would generate an additional $28 trillion in gross domestic product (GDP) by 2025. McKinsey defines a full potential scenario as one where women and men contribute to and participate equally in the economy. Looking specifically at North America, they estimate an increase of 19 percent in annual GDP if gender equality is fully realized.[6] As a business manager or owner, can you really afford to leave your slice of a potential $3.1 trillion pie on the table?

Let's look at this from another, more specific angle and take it down to the level of individual businesses. In a study of over 22,000 businesses, the Peterson Institute of International Economics found that companies with at least 30 percent female executives rake in as much as six percentage points more in profits.[7] Looking at results like this, it's clear that achieving gender parity at a basic employee level isn't enough. Companies need to institute standards and programs to help ensure men and women have equal access to leadership positions. If women are earning more than half of all undergraduate degrees and represent half of the workforce, doesn't it seem odd that they occupy less than 20 percent of major leadership positions across the board? Studies like the Peterson Institute's are helping put empirical data to the problem, raising awareness, and giving life to strategies for improvement.

Some countries in the EU have instituted quotas for female representation on corporate boards and in the C-suite. While I have suggested that companies set individual standards for themselves, I disagree with diversity being mandated by law. While it may work in some cases for those companies already sympathetic to the efforts to achieve gender diversity, these types of laws also have the potential to backfire and create hostility and distrust.

It's a bit like being forced to play with your next-door neighbor as a kid. Neither party wants to be put in that awkward situation, and everyone walks away from it unhappy. With these types of quotas, despite hiring very qualified women, there are some people who would approach it with the belief that women in these positions were given the role to satisfy the letter of the law—to get the feds off their backs—not because they've earned it. It's neither a fair nor accurate judgment, but it's the reality of the world at large.

It seems far more effective to promote the economic benefits of diversity as a proven incentive. Any company worth its salt and interested in long-term profit and success will recognize the value and importance of diversity and adjust accordingly.

Now, I can foresee some critics reading the education statistics and pointing out that I neglected to mention that women are currently earning only 18 percent of computer science degrees, compared to 37 percent in the 1980s (see Figure 7.3).

How can we improve gender diversity ratios in technology fields if women aren't pursuing science, technology,

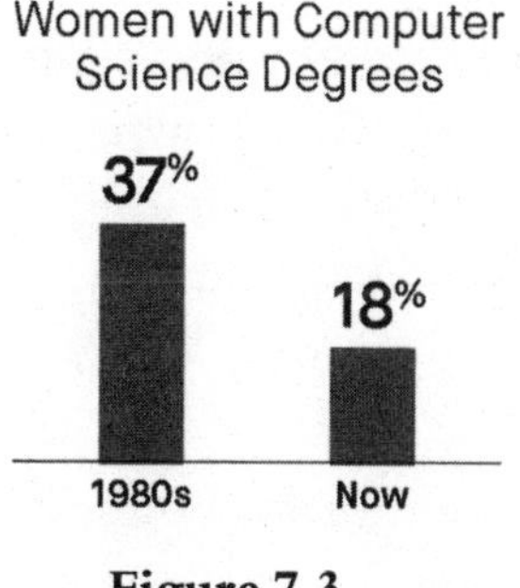

Figure 7.3

engineering, and mathematics (STEM) degrees? I'll leave the answer to that in the very capable hands of Lindsey Armstrong, COO of InsideSales.com.

Want to See More Women in Tech? It's About Aspiration

Who do you think of when you think about the technology world? Steve Jobs? Mark Zuckerberg? Geeks in hoodies who can't look you in the eye or hold a sensible social conversation? Not many girls think "that's exactly who I want to be."

You want gender diversity? It starts with aspiration. If girls don't aspire to be "like" something, they won't ever "be" that something.

If we consistently communicate that technology equals computer science and that computer science equals men, then computer science will always equal a bro culture characterized by developers with a superiority complex and reputation for not welcoming women into their midst.

Current prevailing sentiment promotes STEM as the meaningful educational foundation for the technology industry; right-brain–focused subjects to deliver logic and innovation.

But what about the *art* of technology?

There's beauty in a line of code. Certainly, technologists swoon over great code in the same way I might love the prose of F. Scott Fitzgerald. They see shape and form, style and signature. They see the clever twists in the execution of the design; they see a seamless whole created by a team of individuals working in harmony.

And what of the way technology now permeates the fabric of all our lives, every day? Of the billions of clicks women make to pay bills, buy goods, find answers, and connect and communicate, almost everything they use wasn't built with them in mind. It wasn't designed *for* them.

You would never assume that women would just buy men's clothes. You would rightly assume that making women's clothes especially for them was a good idea likely to lead to a thriving business. And you would probably start by hiring women who could help the menswear designers and manufacturers see a different point of view. We should take the same approach with technology.

So who best represents this new technology leader; who are these next generation role models?

Look at Natalie Massanet, founder of Net-a-Porter.com (sold to Yoox in 2015). One of the smartest, chicest women on the planet, a former fashion model and stylist turned business leader. An English Literature grad. What is Net-A-Porter? Technology, not fashion.

Or Martha Lane Fox (now Baroness Lane-Fox of Soho), another brilliant, stylish and funny woman, creator of a business model that forever changed the leisure industry, who read ancient and modern history at Oxford. She (with Brent Hoberman) founded Lastminute.com, a disruptive technology platform, not a travel site. What girl wouldn't want to be just like them?

These women are innovators who have significantly shaped how we interact online; compelling business leaders with the vision and courage to disrupt and change the tech industry.

They are arts graduates, educated to imagine the world from someone else's point of view. Incredibly handy in the tech industry.

STE**A**M, not STEM.

We will only achieve gender diversity in the technology industry when we, as businesses, value STEAM as highly as

(*continued*)

> (*continued*)
>
> STEM. When we as employers value creativity as highly as coding. And when we as managers value women as highly as men.

I'll also say this—I, myself, am an arts graduate. I have a bachelor's in English from Berkeley with an emphasis in Shakespearean literature and I now run a global technology company. Yes, we should encourage young girls to study math and science, but a degree in the humanities isn't a liability. It's an asset, and if we can tap into it effectively, we'll open up another significant wellspring of opportunity and growth.

ORGANIZATIONAL BENEFITS OF GENDER DIVERSITY

Apart from the economic benefits of gender diversity, there are numerous other advantages that businesses can experience. I'd like to first discuss some of the reasons why we prefer familiarity over diversity and then dive into the benefits of fighting that impulse.

Why We Are Drawn to the Familiar

A homogeneous population is defined as one that is made up of the same kind of people or things. In other words, the group shares more similarities than differences. We, as people, are drawn toward others who are similar to us. We are comforted by the familiar and naturally seek it out, whether those similarities are physical or mental. (It's important to note that what is familiar isn't always the healthiest, smartest, or safest choice.)

Every occupation is stressful on some level, and since we are programmed to seek out familiarity for comfort to combat that stress, it's not surprising that we are naturally inclined to work with similar people. This inclination leads to the formation of homogeneous groups, even among companies that pride themselves on innovation. However, we also know diversity is a prominent driver of innovation, so despite the fact that stress triggers a need for familiarity, it's important to diversify team structure to keep up the pace. It takes a conscious effort to overcome instinctual triggers, but the benefits of that diversity extend beyond your bottom line.

Employee Turnover

As I mentioned in the previous chapter, employee turnover can be very costly. According to a series of studies compiled by the Workplace Gender Equality Agency, both men and women are more likely to stay with a company that promotes and practices gender diversity because it is perceived as "fair." Workplaces that support gender diversity also tend to have more flexible work-life balance and family leave policies, things that both sexes value and that increase women's ability to participate equally in the workforce. Lastly, both men and women believe gender-diverse organizations have fair, transparent salary practices, which further increases their trust and desire to stay with those companies.

While I use the terms "perceive" and "believe," that doesn't mean that you can use smoke and mirrors to create the illusion of gender diversity. You have to be honest with your employee culture and commit to the real thing. Otherwise, you can bet the employee culture will sense in a flash any action or signals that undermine the gender diversity commitment you made and it will write you off as just another dishonest, manipulative manager, and a pretty poor one at that.

Improve Access to Target Markets

In the United States, women control or influence 73 percent of all household spending.[8] They aren't just buying on behalf of themselves, but their children, elderly parents, and partners. Even if they aren't the ones clicking the "buy" button, you can bet their opinion has a big effect on that final decision. Since they represent the majority of the general consumer audience, it makes sense to include women on the teams responsible for selling to them.

Pursuing gender diversity could mean the difference between a business faux pas like Bic offering a new line of pink pens for women, and the success of Nike's latest ad campaigns that focus on the strength, competition, and drive of both men and women in sports and fitness. Diverse teams naturally put checks and balances in place, helping to guard against thoughtlessness toward their audience. Getting input from women about their own experiences and those of other women can enhance the empathy of your campaigns, creating a deeper, more effective customer connection.

Enhance Reputation

If your business is recognized for gender diversity, it can have a positive impact on recruiting and attracting new clients. Valuing gender diversity doesn't just communicate that you value women, but that you value fairness and equality across all aspects of your business. This enhanced reputation can lead to more meaningful relationships with your current customers, prospects, partners, and employees.

Men Benefit, Too

Studies have shown attitudes that inhibit gender diversity in the workplace have a negative impact for both men and women.

The viewpoints that can prevent women from being hired or from moving up in a company are the same perspectives that can limit the work-life flexibility for men in the same office.

Men with children increasingly have partners in the workforce and are taking on more responsibility at home. They cite flexibility as an influential benefit, and companies that offer such flexibility see returns in increased productivity and commitment.

I can say with confidence that almost every man over the age of 35 who has children has experienced some form of censure (spoken or unspoken) from their colleagues when taking time off for the birth of a child or leaving early to attend a sporting event or recital. Thankfully, these attitudes are changing—just look at Mark Zuckerberg setting the example for Facebook employees when he took paternity leave after the birth of his daughter. At Bluewolf, work-life balance and making family a top priority are values we take pride in. I never apologize for adjusting my professional schedule for the needs of my family, and I don't expect my employees to, either.

These flexible policies have a positive impact for every employee and should be embraced by leaders who want to engage with their employees, improve customer connections, and enhance the quality of life they and their employees experience. More than embrace, they should model them wherever appropriate.

Increase Innovation

Anita Woolley, a researcher at Carnegie Mellon University, conducted a study in 2010 on the collective intelligence of groups.[9] She and her team found the overall intelligence of a group wasn't significantly impacted by the individual intelligence of the group members, but by "the average social sensitivity of group members, the equality in distribution of conversational turn-taking, and the proportion of females in the group." While they caution against tokenism, including at least one woman in a group had a significant impact on its collective intelligence.

With the current speed of change, it comes as no surprise that innovation is one of management's top priorities. As I mentioned above, diverse teams enhance creativity and innovation by bringing numerous viewpoints to the discussion. Despite active individual intelligence, groups that occupy the same mind-set have more difficulty expanding beyond their innovation status quo. If you take a look at Figure 7.4, you can see how effective gender diversity is in increasing self-confidence, team efficiency, psychological safety, and team experimentation.

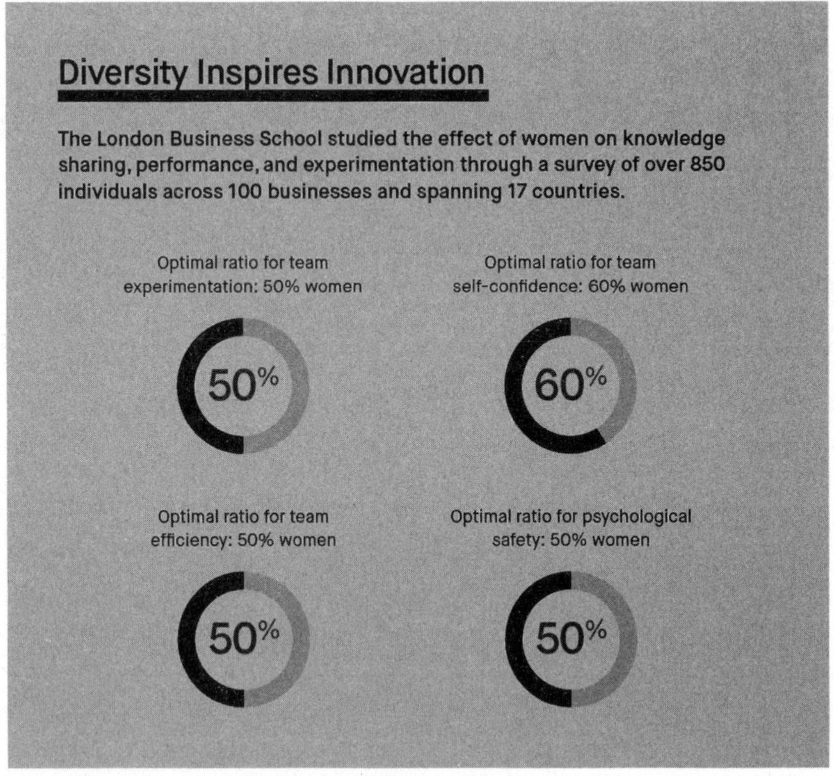

Figure 7.4 London Business School, Innovative Potential: Men and Women in Teams, 2007

Unconscious Bias and Its Effects on Gender Diversity

These days, the word *bias* has a negative connotation, but our biases are what help us make sense of the massive amounts of information we are bombarded by every moment of every day. They help us make split second decisions and guide us through the jungle of our daily lives. For example, if you're a New Yorker and you see a subway car packed with people and the one next to it is empty, you'll choose the crowded car. Why? Because your biases against bad smells, heat, messy spills, and so on caution you to stay away from the empty car. Even if you can't pinpoint exactly what it is, you know something is wrong with that car and you cram yourself into the crowd to avoid it.

Those types of bias are useful to have—they can help you make better decisions, avoid discomfort, pain, and embarrassment, get you somewhere faster, and more. Where our biases fall short is in the people category. Our biases in favor of some people and against others have an overall negative effect on how we hire, fire, promote, and collaborate.

Many of our biases appear innocuous. So what if you prefer Downy over Tide, Southern California over Florida, and extroverts over introverts? How on earth does that affect how you do your job and interact with others at your company? But consider this—I went to Cal, and if I allowed my bias in favor of Berkeley graduates to color my hiring decisions, I would potentially lose out on some incredible candidates. Acknowledging that bias and moving beyond it doesn't mean I can't still mentor undergraduates or contribute to Cal's scholarship fund, but it does mean I can shake off a limitation inhibiting more evenhanded decision making.

The next big question many people wrestle with is whether gender bias really exists. I'm here to tell you it does, and it has a major impact on the number of women we see in leadership positions and on corporate boards, as well as in our general employee makeup. And we are all in this together; women display gender bias just as much as men. The problem is when we encounter it, we have trouble acknowledging that's what it is, even to ourselves.

Let's consider gender bias at the very first level of entry to a company: the hiring process. Numerous studies have proven unconscious gender bias in candidate evaluations.[10]

In one such study, university professors were split into two groups and shown identical résumés with just one minor change—their names. One set of résumés identified the candidate as "John" and the other set "Jennifer." In the results, John was rated significantly higher than Jennifer.[11]

When asked for their reasons for the high or low scores, the professors used identical data to come to different conclusions, such as "John completed three projects last year—that's impressive" and "Jennifer only completed three projects last year—what was she doing with her time?" They never cited gender as a factor, and yet it had a demonstrable effect on their evaluations.

I can see some people asking themselves, "Why does this matter to me? Does the tiny bit of bias that creeps in occasionally really have that big of an effect? Don't my conscious decisions in favor of diversity matter?" And the answer is yes, of course they do. However, it's equally important to be realistic about unconscious bias and the ripple effects that you may not notice on a day-to-day basis.

In an impressive workshop on overcoming unconscious bias in the workplace, Google's director of people analytics, Dr. Brian Welle, cited an interesting study about the impact of gender bias on corporate leadership.[12] Researchers designed a simulation in which an entry-level workforce, 50 percent female and 50 percent male, went through eight levels of evaluations, each time experiencing 15 percent attrition. They randomly assigned them various skills and competency levels and added one final thing: a 1 percent selection bias in favor of men and against women. The researchers ran the simulation 20 times and came up with the same results. By the time this group reached the top rung of the ladder, the split between genders was 35/65 women to men, exactly what we see in business leadership today.

I will say, just as Dr. Welle does, that there are other factors to consider before ascribing the leadership gap solely to unconscious bias. But the fact remains that even a tiny bit of bias can have a far-ranging, cumulative effect on the gender diversity of your teams at all levels, and it's a necessary and worthwhile endeavor to change it.

Strategies to Overcome Gender Bias

There are many methods to overcome bias, but I'd like to focus on three that Dr. Welle covers in his workshop: defining success, collecting data, and accountability.

One of the most effective ways to prevent bias from influencing your hiring decisions and performance evaluations is to define success. Work with your teams and define the specific criteria that you think make a person in that role successful. If you articulate what matters for a role before you review résumés or write that evaluation, you are much less likely to be influenced by any biases. Be fair and be consistent in how you apply those standards, and get your teams involved in the process.

Collecting data is one of the most powerful tools in your arsenal. Remember, you can't improve what you can't measure. Don't phone it in and say gender bias is too hard or too fuzzy to capture. With all of the advanced analytics tools at your fingertips, you have the ability to not just measure your current standing but track your progress against your diversity goals.

Collective, generic info can be used to confirm biases because it's easy to interpret it in the way that seems most favorable. The more ambiguous the information, the more bias can creep in and affect the results or conclusions. For example, some studies have shown that when a review committee is told a group of men and women have done a great job on a project and are given a list of each team member's accomplishments, there is no bias, and congratulations and positive reviews are spread evenly across the team. However, if these specifics are withheld and the committee is simply told that the team did well, they are less likely to rate the women on the project as having done as well as the men. Success is ascribed to the male members of the group, and the women are assumed to have contributed less.

Some of the most readily available data—how many women are on your project teams, working as developers, engineers, and managers, and the entire company ratio of men to women—can give you a very solid starting point. Then, take a deeper look at your business to discover what else you can measure to help counteract bias. It can be anything from the gender representation at leadership retreats and conferences to how sales leads are routed among your teams. It very well may be that in some of these areas, you're doing well. The point here is not to assume compliance with your gender diversity standards, but to objectively measure your standing and target areas for improvement.

The last strategy I recommend using to combat unconscious bias is accountability. This goes beyond accountability for the measurable goals discussed above. I am asking you to embed accountability into your day-to-day actions. When you make a decision about anything, from your project team makeup or written review to new hire, discuss the reasoning behind your choices. This would preferably take place with another person, but it's also very effective to write it down for yourself. By consistently reviewing your actions and openly acknowledging your reasons and motivations, you can cut down on bias significantly.

That same standard of accountability should be applied across your organization. Make a point to hold your employees accountable for the decisions they make. If you can't have an open discussion about the challenges, opportunities, and achievements in your pursuit of gender diversity, these unconscious biases will not surface and will not change.

How to Achieve Gender Diversity in Your Organization

Achieving gender diversity, like anything worthwhile, takes time and concentrated effort. Here are the top strategies your organization can use to help improve gender diversity.

- Acknowledge unconscious bias and work to break it down. Refer to my advice earlier in this chapter.
- Mentorship: Establishing a mentorship program not only increases social bonding and professional development but also helps even the playing field for men and women as they pursue leadership positions within the company. Taking the time to nurture an employee and his or her career breaks down assumptions, unconscious bias, and increases management's investment in their success. It also helps increase mentees' confidence, business acumen, and leadership potential.
- Data and accountability: As mentioned earlier, data can be your best friend as you work toward gender diversity. Find out where you stand, establish goals, and set standards to hold yourself and your teams accountable for achieving them.
- Parental leave: If your company doesn't already have a paid leave policy, seriously consider implementing one. Research has shown that people who work for companies with paid leave policies are more likely to return to work and stay with the company longer. If you think you can only afford a short leave, consider offering on-site day care so new parents can return to work but still take care of their children.
- Work-life balance: Life happens. Your kids get sick; they make it unexpectedly to the championship game happening

at four o'clock on a Thursday; you forget to sign a permission slip and have to turn around to drop it off at school. Be flexible and strongly communicate that policy throughout all levels of your organization. Make it an integral part of your culture and you'll reap the benefits in terms of productivity and commitment.

- Standardize your hiring process: Define success criteria, create a standard set of questions to ask candidates (question set can vary depending on position), and make it a group decision (see accountability discussed previously).

One very important point to remember is these efforts need to encompass your entire business. Gender diversity won't have the impact you expect or desire if you achieve a 50/50 ratio of male and female employees, but all of the women are concentrated in one or two departments.

Lastly, don't insulate yourself or your efforts. Partner with or found a group whose primary goal is to support women in business. As I've said repeatedly throughout this chapter, and the entire book, collaboration and diverse teams help us innovate faster and more effectively. If it holds true for an individual organization, it certainly applies to the professional community at large.

In 2015, there was an increasing number of panels and organizations focused on women in business, which is heartening to see, but just seven years ago, these events were fewer and farther in between. Mindful of that deficit, Corinne Sklar, Bluewolf's CMO, founded the Women Innovators Network (WIN), a community that highlights and promotes women as entrepreneurs and innovators. WIN celebrates, encourages, and supports female leaders who are driving business excellence and success at all levels and in all departments.

The highlight of WIN is its annual networking and awards night at Dreamforce. At the event, Bluewolf organizes a panel of female executives to host a roundtable discussion about pressing issues, challenges, and opportunities for women in business. Open to both men and women, the event fosters the development of new ideas to improve gender diversity, women's leadership opportunities, and collaboration between all attendees, male and female. WIN's goal is to create a strong, connected community of advocates for women in technology and business leadership.

Without cross-collaboration, efforts to improve opportunities for women won't succeed, which is why I am so committed to this organization's impact and success. What began as a small group with high-minded ideals and big goals has turned into an influential network of over 200 female executives and entrepreneurs dedicated to making a difference in their industries.

Change happens through many voices, and organizations like WIN help amplify them. The more we are heard, the more constructive discussions we can engage in, the closer we are to realizing our gender diversity goals.

From a practical perspective, I strongly believe companies with balanced genders perform at a much higher level than those that don't. In our hypercompetitive, resource-constrained world, a gender-balanced business has a much better chance to succeed than one that operates with an uneven ratio favoring men over women.

I know this because I have worked with women and men in the tech space for 24 years. I know this because I have listened to experts in this field whose research supports gender diversity and equality. I know this because I have watched incredible things occur repeatedly when men and women work together. It's that simple. My first job out of college was on Oracle's inside sales team. Back then, our gender diversity ratio was progressively high, as I recount the colleagues on my team. And that team performed at the highest levels in the software industry. I don't hold an advanced degree in human behavior, but it's clear to me that men and women bring different qualities and approaches to collaboration. I have seen my share of disasters when a room, project, or a company is overloaded by one gender. Whether it's a leadership team, a sales call, or complex enterprise transformation, I am convinced a balanced team wins every time.

Bluewolf was cofounded 15 years ago by two men: Michael Kirven and me. But our first hires were women. Our decisions weren't based on gender, but because we had worked with them successfully in prior companies. Our company growth skyrocketed as we hired our first sales directors, Caryn Fried and Lexy Werner; our VP of delivery, Jolene Chan; and our VPs of recruiting, Stephany Samuels and Wendy Duarte. All of these women are senior leaders in our company to this day, and the list is deeper than space allows here. They have been married, relocated, reorganized; they have had children; they have hired and mentored hundreds of employees; they have contributed to our business in their own unique and incredible ways.

Gender diversity is an incredibly powerful asset for any company. Great ideas, great work, and unbelievable results come out of melting pots. It is time to stop hiding behind our fears on this topic. We need to give it transparency, speak in real terms and relevant language, and make gender diversity—and in turn, equality—our primary and common goal.

8

Right Time, Right Moment, Right Channel

If you're a manager, improving customer service can be a costly, painful initiative. Even if your defining business strategy is to be a customer-focused organization, the nitty-gritty details of delivering traditional customer service pose many potential obstacles—the kind delivered by reps working in a call center who service very vocal clientele—which is absolutely *not* what you love about being a customer-focused organized.

And when you think of customer service *as* a customer, you probably don't have the nicest view of it, primarily because you tend to only call customer service with a problem. However, the customer service landscape is changing rapidly, and it's due to two important factors. One, companies have started to pay closer attention to their customers' wants, needs, and quality of experience. Two, service technology has now caught up to the dreams and visions of even the most customer obsessed business.

Now, companies who want to deliver high-quality experiences and turn customer problems on their heads have access to a suite of integrated technology that makes their reps' lives easier and their customers happier.

This suite of customizable tools is exactly what the Midwest Operating Engineers Welfare Fund (MOE) used to improve the day-to-day experiences of their members and employees. MOE is the organization tasked with providing healthcare benefits to roughly 23,000 actively working and 10,000 retired Local 150 member families. Local 150 is a labor union representing operating engineers that work in a variety of construction related industries, such as road building, mass earth moving, pits and quarries, landfills, drilling, material testing, concrete pumping, and railroad, pipeline, landscaping, public works, and heavy equipment mechanics throughout Northern Illinois, Northern Indiana, and seven counties in Southeastern Iowa.

As is typical with labor unions, MOE had a single healthcare plan option for most of the actively working members it services. This ultimately meant that there was no real difference in the healthcare provided to a single member who is 25-years-old versus a middle-aged man with a family of five. After the passing of the Affordable Care Act, healthcare costs have continued to rise at an alarming rate for both MOE and the union members, so the one-size fits all healthcare plan was no longer effective. As a result, the MOE Board of Trustees developed a progressive plan to provide its members with a new set of healthcare plan options that can meet their families' needs, while trying to drive down the rising costs it faces on a yearly basis. Subsequently, the MOE Health Plan Marketplace was born, a healthcare exchange for Local 150 members.

In addition to the efforts to combat the increased healthcare costs, the MOE and Local 150 had yet to embrace a true digital process; thousands of dollars were being spent on postage and correspondence through the mail. Union fees had to be paid in person or sent in using snail mail, requiring some members to drive over three hours just to pay their dues or update their personal information. The entire Local 150 organization had a strong desire to cut costs, more efficiently manage the healthcare process, and ultimately provide a better experience for their members and employees.

MOE and Local 150 first worked with Salesforce, and upon Salesforce's recommendation, Bluewolf, to create an integrated, digital, branded community that would allow members to manage their benefits online. Bluewolf helped gather and define the requirements necessary to integrate the current technology the organizations were using on the Salesforce platform and construct the MOE Health Plan Marketplace.

In less than nine months, the "My150" employee and member community was born. Powered by Salesforce Service Cloud on the back end and branded with Community Cloud on the front end, the new community is now a one-stop-shop for the MOE Health Plan Marketplace. MOE worked to create the MOE Health Plan Marketplace consisting of seven health plan options that provide coverage to meet the diversified members' medical needs, each at different price points (known as credits). MOE and Bluewolf collaborated to provide members with a custom 'Wizard' feature to assist members in navigating to a health plan option that fit their medical needs. They also developed a custom "Affordability Calculator" that lets members plug in their estimated hours of work to determine if their health plan selection is affordable for their family based on their anticipated amount of hours in the upcoming season and their Credit Bank balance.

Additionally, using My150, members can now review general account information, manage dependents, review FAQs, submit benefit questions on-line and pay membership dues online, as opposed to doing paperwork and submitting forms and payments in person—ultimately trying to provide members an easy self-service tool to utilize.

MOE and Local 150's members spend most of their mental and physical energy on the jobsite. The last thing they should have to wrestle with during their off-hours are the healthcare benefits that are vital to their peace of mind and safety. To help with adoption of the new online platform, the MOE administration team traveled to their members, assisting them with sign ups in person and learning about the new MOE Health Plan Marketplace. Their priority was making enrollment as easy as possible, and they continue to dedicate significant time and effort in supporting their members on the platform. Since the site launched in October 2015, over 11,000 members have signed up, resulting in significant savings and a much better experience. What's more, this is a living, breathing platform that is able to grow and change with the entire organization.

MOE and Local 150's innovative experience offers a stark contrast between the traditional customer service of the past and today's modern omnichannel customer service, which has emerged as the command center for the customer voice.

You could sum up the difference, which we call the Bluewolf Customer Covenant, like this: I (your customer) will give you my information, but in return you must know me—and know me with all the details correct, up to date, and consistent—across all channels and regardless of the particular agent. In short, service channels can change, agents can change, and data can change, but whoever is handling my service in that instance should know me without my having to describe the same problem or situation over and over again.

This isn't as hard to achieve now as it was even a few years ago, due in large part to the adoption of social business and better cloud-based systems and data integration tools. With the amount of data and service channel options available now (mobile, social, communities, phone, e-mail, chat, and more), it is not only essential to have a quality service center that can deliver a consistent omnichannel experience but it is also remarkably simple. Technology can take over the heavy lifting of the past: grabbing the right data from a smattering of different systems, combining it into a single view of the customer, and then putting it in front of the service agent on the phone or online with that customer. If you want to get a little more sophisticated or you're not confident your service agents will do a good job, you can embed rules-based logic into the system that will walk your agent through the call with data-supported prompts at every point along the way. Suddenly, customer-appropriate and well-informed cross selling and upselling can be handled by any service agent.

Social customer service plays a big part. As I mentioned previously, many customer surveys report that growing numbers of people, especially among the most highly sought younger demographics, increasingly prefer to handle their customer services needs via social channels. At Bluewolf, we expect this tendency to only grow and expand going forward. As a result, companies that intend to remain relevant must extend their customer service into the social space. It is not, however, a choice of adding social while cutting the call center or online self-service. In the new age of omnichannel service, all service channels will remain viable. Customers repeatedly tell researchers they use different service channels at different times and for different needs. Woe to the manager who thinks the company can save money by eliminating one of them.

In fact, today's customers are increasingly turning to social media to connect with a brand's customer service department. For consumers, however, dissatisfaction still remains. In one study, over 50 percent of consumers wanted a response on social media within two hours (Figure 8.1);[1] yet in another, two-thirds reported they needed to reach out at least twice to get a response (Figure 8.2).[2]

Companies need to invest in tools, processes, and integrations to fix this, mainly by prioritizing these conversations and supporting their customers the way they want to be supported. That most likely means going the omnichannel route.

Did I say omnichannel? There is a debate raging in the customer service industry around multichannel and omnichannel. They are

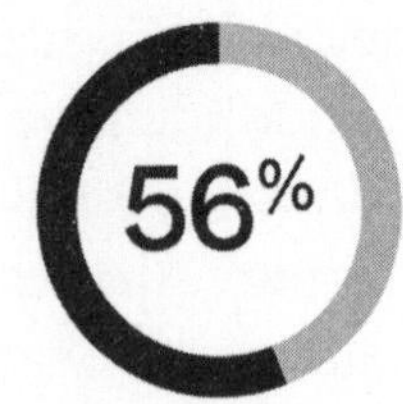

Figure 8.1 Social Customer Service Performance Report June 2013, Hubspot

Figure 8.2 "The State of Customer Service Experience 2015," The Northridge Group

effectively the same thing, but the debate continues. From my standpoint, I agree with Fred Astaire and Ginger Rogers in *Shall We Dance*: "You say tomato and I say tomahto," and if we're talking about the same thing, what does it matter? The same goes for multichannel and omnichannel. They both entail fully integrating all the service channels so the customer has a singular service experience no matter how the service is delivered. That's what the Bluewolf Customer Covenant mentioned previously is about.

Reportedly, the debate between multichannel and omnichannel came about due to the slow adoption of multichannel servicing, which was exacerbated by the lack of integration between servicing applications. Application and data integration wasn't easy or cheap a few years back. Companies would invest in integration and finally get it working right, and something would change—new technology or new data formats and interfaces. Then the company would have to do the integration all over again. Innovative companies that were willing to spend money on their service organizations added new channels or whatever was needed. But even they missed the importance of creating a frictionless customer experience and instead established siloed groups to handle each one. Big mistake.

We see this all the time. If a customer first sends an e-mail and then calls, the phone agent has no way of finding out what happened on the alternative channel, forcing customers to start over every time (see Figure 8.3). That's why we came up with the Bluewolf Customer Covenant. As different regions of the world continue to lag in adoption of myriad servicing channels, the lack of a fully integrated servicing environment remains a major issue. Other vendors have said "the hell with it," found a way to handle the integration more easily, and called it omnichannel to emphasize their difference. Whatever term you choose, it's clear companies that can seamlessly integrate customer data across current and future channels can maintain a distinctive service advantage.

Another expert, Donna Fluss, put it this way: "Vendors explain that the difference between multichannel and

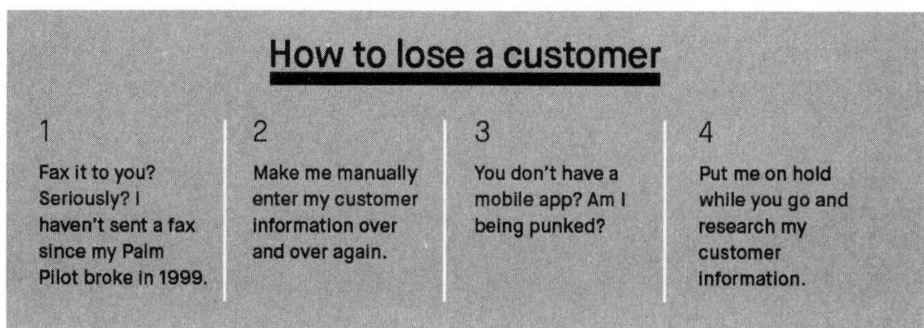

Figure 8.3

omnichannel is that the former is a failed concept and the latter is an unsullied one with great potential."[3] That's just what a vendor would say, especially one that wants to sell an old idea under a new name. But Fluss sees through this: "In the world of 'buzz,' *multi* and *omni* are virtually interchangeable." For the purposes of this book and simplicity, I will use omnichannel; feel free to use either as long as you understand we're talking about the same things. And if you use multichannel, I assure you I will know what you mean.

So let's take a moment to recap what those various service channels specifically are, starting with the traditional service channels:

- Snail mail (U.S. Postal Service)
- Voice telephone
- E-mail
- Fax
- SMS
- Chat

Neither snail mail nor fax are amenable to the added capabilities that digital systems provide since they are not inherently digital.

The new digital service channels include:

- Social
- Web
- Video/YouTube
- Mobile app
- Online portal/Communities
- Client service app

Taken together, these constitute a lot of channels. Too many, in fact. You don't, however, need to address all of them, only the ones your customers actually use.

Channel integration is crucial to the success of the omnichannel customer experience, but you have to prioritize the right channels, not try to use every channel. For our purposes you can skip snail mail and fax. Then figure out where your customers are today and enable them to interact with you there. At the same time, sales, marketing, and service all need the same visibility and should work together. Remember the customer covenant; you don't want different groups servicing the customer based on different (and not necessarily current) information. Finally, don't downplay the importance of social media in all of this.

BRIDGING CUSTOMER SERVICE AND SOCIAL

Tired of long hold times and unanswered e-mails? Then join the folks who are increasingly turning to social media to connect with a brand's customer service department. Many will still be disappointed by what they find because many companies still lack the tools and integrations to prioritize these conversations and adequately support their customers. You will still find companies that haven't managed to bolster their social management capabilities or enrich their case management process to deliver a better customer experience.[4]

Unfortunately, many companies still centralize their social media management. That was okay when social media was new and many people in the organization lacked experience with it. That left social media management exclusively in the hands of marketing or corporate communications teams, who were thought to have the most social media experience. To prevent any embarrassing public faux pas, the company voice was controlled by a select few. Companies didn't trust just any employee talking to customers, even though it might be that very employee who actually had the expertise to address their issues. Fortunately, things have started to change.

Now, in a world where Facebook alone has over one billion users, almost everybody has some experience with social media. On top of that, organizations with a strong social presence and high engagement are waking up to the realization that certain customer posts aren't always best answered by a marketer. Depending on the issue, it might be someone in tech support or sales who knows how to handle the customer in that particular case. As a result, the best organizations today utilize a robust social listening platform that automatically flags which department, and even which individual, should handle a particular social media post.

For example, if a customer posts a complaint about a product, a customer service ticket is automatically generated and assigned to a trained customer service agent for response and resolution. If a customer posts a question about a competitor, the message might be better directed to a salesperson who can explain how the organization differentiates itself from competitors. At the same time, the company must also consider integration and automation of their social management to produce the most seamless and consistent customer experience possible, even if different people are handling different issues for the same customer. This is important because in the end it is the *same* customer no matter how many different people have responded. Every person who responds should have the same accurate data and know what is going on without the customer having to go back to the beginning or even repeat a few steps. Repetition is the antithesis of a good customer experience.

This is where top-notch data integration becomes important. The goal is to combine social data with all the other data and make it accessible to all—not just sales and service, but with training, accounting, tech support, and anyone else who might touch the customer and impact their experience. Doing this will provide a more complete view of your customers' behavior across channels, sales cycle velocity and opportunity influences, customer engagement, and more. Marketers used to refer to this as a 360-degree view, but that doesn't even begin to capture the degree of seamlessness, comprehensiveness, and integration you want. You need to invest in dashboards that integrate social behavioral data with relevant sales, service, and marketing data about a particular customer. Don't forget accounting data, particularly payables, receivables, and credit balances to address questions about payment or billing. And you'd better include data from training and support tickets, too, should a technical issue arise.

I hope I've made my point: If you are committed to following the Bluewolf Customer Covenant, all of your people, whether in customer service or not, need to be able to access all the data about the customer, because you never know what issue is going to come up or who is going to handle it in that moment. And remember, your customer service is measured against the customer's last best experience.

COMMUNITIES

Online customer self-service used to be simple. Just post an online FAQ—short or long, it hardly mattered—and customers would read it to find the info they wanted. If you were inspired to get fancy, especially if you posted a long FAQ, you add could add an index or search capabilities to make it easier.

Those were the good old days. Now, online customer service goes far beyond just trying to find the right answer to your question. It is about being able to actively collaborate with employees, partners, and other customers to create new solutions. This has the potential to radically change the customer service experience for you, your partners, and most of all for your customers. You're already customer focused. Now you not only have customers but customer-partners; it is a totally new dynamic that you will need to manage differently. It raises a host of issues ranging from ownership of the resulting intellectual property to revenue distribution.

As the availability of customer service contact channels increases, customers also are engaging with nontraditional, digital service options as often, if not more, than their traditional service agent counterparts. In 2015—for the first time ever—web self-service surpassed telephone service as the number one customer service channel among U.S. adults.[5]

In the contact center, a move to self-service can create a different set of growing pains. Customer service organizations accustomed to traditional service channels might balk at a more informal, networked approach to serving their customers. Often, I suspect, the aversion to greater informality is a cover for resistance to change and even a concern over job security. The good news is the shift to self-service pays off: self-service and communities give customers greater access to information that is immediate, insightful, and—in some cases—emotional, building connection and creating customer loyalty. You may even find customers helping other customers with a given issue. In the context of striving to be customer focused and delivering an outstanding customer experience, emotion can be a powerful, yet often overlooked, aspect. As Forrester Research put it, "companies work hard to improve customer experience (CX) but often emphasize its utilitarian aspects of effectiveness and ease rather than emotion—how interactions make customers feel."[6]

At Bluewolf, we've seen companies that take advantage of cloud-based communities as part of their self-service strategy reap huge benefits. Bluewolf's 2015 *The State of Salesforce* report

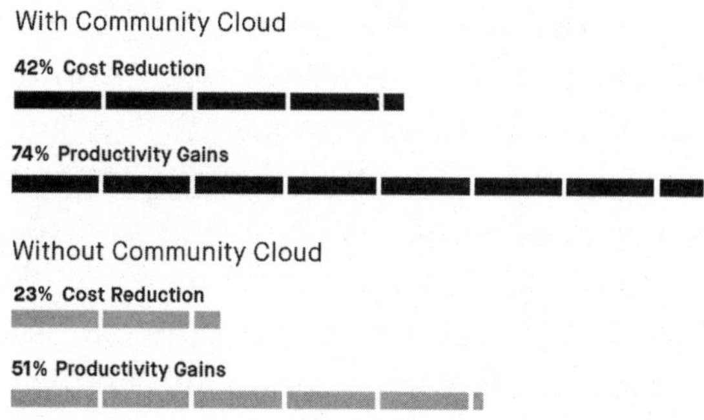

Figure 8.4 The State of Salesforce 2015–2016

showed that 42 percent of companies using communities reported reduced costs and 74 percent reported productivity gains compared to those not utilizing it, who reported 23 percent and 51 percent in the same categories (see Figure 8.4).

The shift to a more agile, customer-obsessed enterprise with cloud-based communities starts with determining what drives your organization by asking questions like, what are the goals for the community you're creating? How will users interact with it?

Unlike service agents, who often have no choice but to work with complicated systems, customers will quickly abandon a user interface that is confusing or doesn't provide immediate value. It's imperative that your portals and communities are easy to use, include accessible and accurate content along with context-sensitive help, and are mobile enabled. Bob Furniss, Bluewolf's service practice director gives four steps that will help you make this shift to sustainable and beneficial self-service portals and communities:

1. Invest in the user experience. One example is Facebook's community, which delivers value to its members through its effortless user interface and user experience (UI/UX); its participants, not the provider, create the value of its current user experience. An excellent, easy-to-use UI/UX

creates the positive first impressions that drive successful onboarding and a sense of ownership. Of all the users of a knowledge portal, customers have the least tolerance for a poor user experience and will abandon it before they ever become practiced with it. While agents have to navigate the knowledge portal every day, customers are likely looking up something for the first time. Bring the same level of intention to the creation of your community as you would to launching your company website.

2. Appoint a team of community champions. A community provides a central place for its audience to engage. Dedicate a team of individuals who are responsible for continually driving engagement from the community members. Don't sit back and think engagement will grow organically—it may, but it will take too long. Consider including a collaborative communication component to communities. Whether your strategy is focused on internal audiences, external audiences, or both, effective communication is the best way to drive greater levels of engagement.
3. Make content king. If self-service is one of your strategies, content is as important as user experience. If you're creating a self-service portal, ensure that content is accessible and integrated into the community. Don't build a community or self-service portal as a stand-alone product. Expose your audience to valuable information that will drive ROI as they use it. It is often beneficial to create pathways to promote and increase the visibility of knowledge that has proven helpful in case resolution. Make sure every knowledge article has an expiration date and periodically review all content and update when necessary. Allow agents to flag cases that require self-service content, thus alerting the knowledge team and proactively showing customers the knowledge they need to help themselves.

4. Remember that mobile self-service is the new standard. Consider ways to enable mobile case management. With smartphone usage in the United States nearing 80 percent, mobile is becoming customers' preferred medium for support.[7] Mobile self-service is quickly becoming the hallmark of forwarding-thinking leaders in customer service. No matter what industry you are in or what your community use case is, your organization needs to plan for how your consumers will use it on the go.[8]

I'll tack onto the end of Bob's steps to remind you to embrace *all* customer feedback, positive or negative. Companies who handle customer problems smoothly and efficiently often turn dissatisfied users into loyal evangelists. For example, one of my employees shared with me her experience with USAA (banking and insurance for military families) on Twitter. After watching a commercial that featured only male soldiers, she mentioned them in a tweet encouraging them to recognize all service members, male and female, in their advertisements. Less than 24 hours later, USAA responded to her, thanked her for her feedback, and said they would remake the ad to better represent the entirety of the service member community. When I asked her whether they followed through, she was very happy to report that they had. It's that type of responsiveness that creates deep customer relationships. Aim for success, but take any failures and do everything you can to course correct and turn them to your advantage to better serve your customers.

CALL CENTERS STILL MATTER

Digital technology, as powerful and innovative as it is, especially when communicating and engaging with customers faster than ever before, does not mean the end of the call center. The power

Figure 8.5 "The Economic Necessity of Customer Service," Forrester Research

of traditional channels such as the call center shouldn't be underestimated. In fact, research from Forrester found that 50 percent of web transactions are still completed with the help of an agent, and many customers will go elsewhere if this is not a smooth interaction (Figure 8.5).[9]

The customer desire and expectation of having the option to talk with a live agent wherever and whenever they need it means that call centers remain a central hub that continues to shape customer experience. However, with the rise of cloud technology, businesses often shift to focus on the technology implementation of their call centers while mistakenly ignoring the fundamentals of customer service, which devalues the very purpose for which the call center was created in the first place.

In general, I downplay the importance of technology implementation in favor of focusing on the people involved. One of the biggest mistakes businesses make is building a call center based on technology specifications rather than on people issues and business objectives. When building or reengineering a call center, organizations must begin by defining the goals of the call center and how its success will be measured. Questions like "What am I actually trying to achieve with this call center?" and "Why is it important to the company?" should be asked long before "How will it be delivered?" How it gets delivered may change multiple times over the next few years.

The most successful call centers are those that have clear business goals, such as:

- Drive higher rates of return by proactively engaging existing customers with helpful information about their product
- Establish a customer-centric culture by putting theory into practice
- Boost net promoter score (NPS) to drive brand awareness and new customer sales
- Manage more customer inquiries by outsourcing case management to the customer community
- Focus on becoming an industry leader in sales and service by providing an amazing customer experience across all relevant channels

In short, technology and rapid development should not be confused with building a leading customer engagement strategy. Technology is only an enabler; without a strong strategic foundation to guide and inform development, your company will not achieve its business outcomes.

CUSTOMER SERVICE EXCELLENCE, NOT CASE MANAGEMENT

The true nature of customer engagement lies in understanding what a customer needs before they know they need it—not just resolving cases as they arise. It certainly isn't easy to know how to proactively engage your customers, but analytics and triggers can constantly monitor customer behavior and predict when a customer is about to have an issue. These tools can alert agents to proactively reach out to a customer before the issue arises, or even communicate directly with the customer. Product or service incidents are inevitable, but going to your customers with a solution before they even know they have a problem is a great way to show them you are on top of things and you care.

Furthermore, knowledge-centered support allows your team to create valuable content as a byproduct of solving customer issues. Since agents are increasingly using content to solve customer issues, consider moving toward customer self-service by making that knowledge public facing. When content is external, you allow your community of customers to enhance and improve the knowledge for you.

It may sound simple, but the most successful businesses are those that are customer focused or, as we say at Bluewolf, customer obsessed. Being able to count on a call center to provide an agent who is understanding, efficient, and armed with the right information and tools is much more valuable to a customer than being rushed through a call in under 60 seconds. It's the focus on the individual customer (or lack thereof) that will make all the difference.

Ultimately, the purpose of a call center shouldn't be forgotten. Whether solving problems before a customer even knows they're there, answering queries, or making customers feel valued through completely personalized communications, the call center is there to drive customer engagement, loyalty, and sales.

While you're planning your call center, please take note of the following three mistakes to avoid:

1. Building a contact center from technology specs instead of business outcomes. Start by defining the goals of the contact center and how success will be measured. The most successful contact centers start a project by setting clear business outcomes.

2. Building a contact center purely for case management. The true nature of customer engagement lies in understanding what a customer needs before they know they need it—not just resolving cases as they arise. It certainly isn't easy to know how to proactively engage your customers, but one easy way to get started fast is by building a community for your customers to engage with each other and product experts from your team, and reward or recognize collaboration and contribution. Most important, don't fear the potential for negative conversation. If your clients want to say something negative about your product or service, then you should want to hear it! Better you hear it from them first than hear about it later on Facebook.
3. Focusing on cost-per-call stats rather than on customer effort and experience. This one is simple to avoid: always be customer obsessed. Your agents should be committed to delivering a quality experience rather than worrying about completing 60 calls in 60 minutes.

In addition, remember to regularly update your knowledge management and continuously grow it. Without knowledge management, and especially knowledge about the customer, the management platform won't reach its full potential. Accelerate and enable the goal of "right time, right moment, right channel."

Finally, reporting remains a key focus in all contact centers. Companies need to be able to track the entire customer journey, not just the vertical channels. Case management plays a big part in this success.

The last thing I want to emphasize before moving on to the next chapter is to remember who the agent is. While it's often the call center agents, it's not *only* them. Everyone who touches the customer, no matter their role, is the agent at that point of contact and needs to own the moment. That means empowering every employee, service agent or otherwise, with a quality knowledge base so they can fulfill the Bluewolf Customer Covenant. Empowering employee engagement with the right data via the right channel leads to better customer engagement and, ultimately, a better customer experience.

9

Turning Data into Action

Big data as an information technology (IT) strategy has been around for a decade or longer. Remember when it was data mining? When companies set up data warehouses and data marts? One witty analyst referred to data convenience stores; maybe he should have called it "little data." Regardless of what you call it, it's no secret that big data presents both an opportunity and a challenge. And there is another even more important secret about data: It's not about the data, big, little, or in between—it's about business outcomes. The rest of this chapter will talk about data in every possible way, but remember, it is always about the business outcome.

The challenge of big data comes not only from its volume—the world is generating exabytes of new data (by 2016, global IP traffic alone will reach nearly 1 billion gigabytes per month, and will double to 2 billion gigabytes per month by 2019)[1]—but from its velocity, the speed at which it arrives and must be analyzed if it is to deliver any business value. New data is created every second of every day.[2] Given the volume and velocity, it's easy to get lost amid the information.

There are already many strategies to shape and master your data, but the most important ones start with defining the goals and policies around business outcomes: acquisition, retention, cost reduction, and expansion, along with all of the rules governing the use of data. Hopefully, you'll notice that very little of this has to do with the technology itself. Enterprises are moving away from the idea that technology drives company strategy. Instead, business outcomes have reemerged as primary drivers of how organizations prioritize strategic initiatives and enhance digital customer experiences. Whether you become customer driven or not, it's critical that all of your endeavors and investments in the next few years directly affect one or more of these areas—ultimately, they determine the success of your business.

More specifically, Bluewolf's goal is to put every client conversation into the broader context of this question: what outcome is your business looking to drive? Managers can get caught up in and distracted by all of the data suddenly available to them, from social media to the Internet of Things to connected cars and wearable devices. You now have access to more, different, and better data than ever before. So what?

No organization believes in data more than we do at Bluewolf. But here is something to think about: Data is meaningless if you can't define why you need it and how you're going to use it to achieve your objectives. The data itself is worthless without a plan for how you are going to use it. Just like any other piece of technology, it comes down to the strategy behind it that drives success, not the data itself.

THE CHALLENGE OF DATA

If you're this far into this book, you won't be surprised if I say the future of every company depends on customers, not technology. You also shouldn't be surprised if I say you can never know too much about your customer. Now I'm going to add something new: we have entered an era of unlimited data, and the volume is only going to keep growing as more so as more data sources and types of data get added to the mix, arriving faster than ever thought possible. Is your organization prepared to respond in real time to a customer comment made on Facebook from halfway around the world? You could be facing that challenge right now, today, as you read this. To reply by saying, "Good point; let me get back to you tomorrow" probably won't satisfy the customer who posted the comment. This is why you need not only to know why you want this data and how you plan to use it but also to be prepared to use it when the opportunity arrives. You need to understand how to effectively manage and use this increasingly rapid stream of unlimited data and be prepared to respond in real time.

The big data revolution gained significant momentum in 2014, amassing an incomprehensible amount of data: a zettabyte in just the past two years and significantly more by now. Yet the revolution currently under way is not in the unprecedented *quantity* of accumulated data, but the ways in which intelligence is derived from that wealth of information. Salesforce CEO Marc Benioff stated that we are "in the early stages of a data science revolution."

A data science revolution sounds scary, exciting, and mind boggling all at once. The real question for you is what this means for enterprises, particularly your enterprise, and how it will impact your business. My hope, actually my expectation, is that it comes down to achieving predictability, which is the antithesis of scary or mind boggling.

In an ideal world, perfect data science takes every customer interaction and identifies patterns that can be repeated and proactively acted upon. Humans and artificial intelligence systems collaborate in an amalgamation of contextual, timely insight to better understand each customer and, ultimately, to predict their future behaviors. The results won't be flawless—data science is not yet perfect, and scenarios are not necessarily ideal—but this data-based guidance will be accurate enough to give us results that we can almost always depend upon to make the best decisions.

Don't get me wrong; I'm not conjuring up *The Matrix* here; this isn't about that kind of world. Rather, data science will increasingly enable an organization—your organization—to get ahead of a customer's actions, to know what your customers want before they do. This powerful ability is the focal point of business intelligence and customer engagement strategies, since it allows businesses to become more competitive and service oriented, getting them closer to their customers than ever before. In the past, we could only make thoughtful guesses at this and pat ourselves on the back when we got close. Now we can skip the guessing and hit the target almost every single time.

This goes beyond customer service and marketing. The next generation of successful businesses will look to data science to revolutionize their entire organization. The commitment of today's analytics and business intelligence is that data will no longer be isolated to databases, *pulled* by queries in response to an ask, but rather will be integrated throughout an organization's business process layer to predict and *push* prescriptive actions upon employees to take the most relevant and timely next step.

Yet data science is not confined to empowering just the service and customer-facing employees; it cannot exist in a siloed environment. It must be integrated across the entire organization, prompting businesses to realign executives, employees, and processes around the customer and absorb insight-driven value propositions throughout. Design and data science must converge to deliver seamless, relevant, and hyper-integrated customer experiences—across channels, devices, and touch points—to reimagine businesses and their entire workforce. In fact, it will also help organizations to more efficiently manage their workforces, assigning people to tasks they do particularly well but envisioning an entire career path for each individual throughout the organization.

The conversation in today's global market pivots to revolve around not how much data an organization captures, but how it leverages that data to get closer to its customers while maintaining scalability across the enterprise. Data science is the next generation of artificial intelligence and human capability that powers connections between a business and its customers. This isn't black magic, but solid science that can be grasped, tamed, and applied to a wide range of problems managers face all the time. Those who embrace this data science revolution will lead the way to becoming a customer-first business. Those who don't will scramble to play catch-up and wonder how the others did it.

Inside Analytics: Insights from InsideSales Chief Marketing Officer Mick Hollison

EB: There are a ton of conversations going on around data right now, and the first thing I want to address is this concept of predictive. Everyone says predictive, but what does that mean to you?

MH: There's a quote by Spanish philosopher and poet George Santayana that I think is pretty apt for this discussion: "Those who forget history are doomed to repeat it." To me, predictive is about seeing into the future through the lens of the past. What's interesting and new about that—and why it's so important today—is that the advent of big data has made it possible to almost infinitely see into the past, whether that's a past sales interaction or past customer engagement. In the end, predictive is about leveraging past insights to help guide you into the future.

EB: Dialing it back to today, the terms *analytics*, *big data*, and *predictive* are the latest buzzwords. You and I have been around long enough to know that once the buzzwords start hitting, it gets difficult for customers to figure out their true

(*continued*)

(continued)

paths. It's hard for them to make decisions, and business intelligence (BI) and predictive tools have flooded the market. What key attributes should buyers and decision makers take into consideration as they start to make investments in these types of technologies?

MH: The first is painfully apparent, but people love to ignore the obvious, so let's start there. Is the company from whom you're buying tools and tech built to last, or does it just have a new widget that solves a single pain point? Second, infrastructure and security need to be rock solid. InsideSales anonymizes buyer profiles, for example. When you give another company access to your most precious data in the world—your customer data—you have to feel confident in its infrastructure and security. Third, make sure that whoever you buy from has an open platform with a great API set and development kit. Closed or proprietary tech just leads to problems down the line as business complexity increases. Lastly, make sure that the platform you're buying extends to multiple business functions. You don't want to end up with 18 predictive tools solving discrete business problems. The smarter path is to pick a company that is thinking of predictive as more of a platform where the algorithm sets are horizontal enough that they can apply to more business challenges.

EB: Prior to Salesforce, powerful enterprise software was reserved for the privileged few that could afford it and get through a nasty implementation. A big reason that Salesforce took the market by storm was that their product was so easy to buy and use that they flooded the market, drawing in customers of all shapes and sizes. As you look at predictive, do you see a solution like InsideSales or other solutions having that same impact, so that it's truly a democratized offering for organizations? Do you see history repeating itself there?

MH: Yes, absolutely. I think we're going to end up with a predictive app ecosystem, much like what we have with iOS and Android on mobile devices. I'm an Apple user myself, and the reason I'm going to remain one isn't just that it has a beautiful, powerful design; it's the apps. The reason I can't possibly fathom changing, even if somebody came out with faster processors or better screen resolution, is that I'm so wedded to that ecosystem. I believe we're going to end up with a very similar thing here. There are going to be two or three predictive ecosystems with app portfolios that will distinguish those players from anyone else in the marketplace. I would argue that even today that's the competitive motive for Salesforce. Is Microsoft Dynamics just as good of a base CRM? Yes, I think it is. Have they built up the same level of app ecosystem? Not even close. Predictive will become democratized and we're going to have a really rich set of predictive apps, but they're only going to run on top of two or three platforms.

EB: Excellent, that's a great way to look at it. Anything else you want to add, Mick?

MH: In the analytics market, it's definitely still early, and everyone is trying to find their way in terms of predictive. What's really going to separate the men from the boys, aside from an open ecosystem, is who actually has great data to derive great insights. If you don't have a good underlying data set, it's like anything else in computing: garbage in, garbage out. One of the things InsideSales is uniquely positioned with is that we already have over 100 billion sales interactions in our data store, and that number keeps growing. As the number of sales interactions increases, we'll get even more accurate in what we can prescribe. The biggest differentiator beyond the ecosystem front is who's got the best data—and those with the best data are going to win.

DATA INTEGRATION/MIGRATION/ QUALITY—A SALESFORCE RECAP

The following section is primarily Salesforce specific, although the general principles apply to any operation. If you are not a Salesforce shop, feel free to jump ahead to the next section.

Clean data enables better decision making and improves the effectiveness of marketing and sales. It's also a huge commitment to keep your data clean—if not monitored properly, your data will become dirty and less valuable again. So once you've achieved clean data, how do you keep it that way? Here are four strategies to keep your Salesforce data clean.

HOLD EVERY DEPARTMENT RESPONSIBLE

A cross-functional data governance committee is essential to ensure ongoing data quality. All business units should be represented in the committee and collectively own data standards for the company as a whole. According to Bluewolf's *The State of Salesforce* report, 61 percent of organizations surveyed have a group dedicated to cloud governance. Data governance is a core responsibility of every governance team. You don't have to be a Salesforce shop to want to comply with that.

CONSTRAIN DATA INPUT

What do we mean by constraining data input? By using standard Salesforce functionality, you can standardize what users put into Salesforce. Data validation rules, combined with required and unique fields, can limit incorrect information. Ensuring that picklist fields and lookups are used in place of "free text" fields are additional ways to constrain inputs.

A more stringent approach is to create workflow rules that route any newly created customer records to the data governance committee for approval. Only once this approval is granted will the records be committed. This process may look slow and burdensome, but when done well it can be surprisingly efficient and reduce the burden of data cleanup later on.

INTEGRATE WITH TRUSTED DATA SOURCES

Stopping bad data from getting into Salesforce (or any system) is only half the battle. A key challenge for many companies is keeping data up to date. Phone numbers, e-mails, and billing addresses can become outdated surprisingly fast.

Third-party data sources that verify addresses and supplement existing data with demographic data like age, gender, and household income can reduce the burden of entering the data into Salesforce and help correct errors. This applies to non-Salesforce systems as well. The third parties will sell their data to anyone, although the integration may not be as seamless.

These data sources do not have to be external. For example, if a customer can manage their own account information online or by calling into customer service, they can ensure any updated data from the website and service will make it back to the Salesforce account record.

GAMIFY DESIRED BEHAVIORS

The best people to put in charge of keeping the data clean are those who care about the quality of the data. Incentivize those same people with game-like challenges, and data

(*continued*)

(*continued*)

quality will only improve. In other words, data scrubbing and checking is tedious work, so try to make it interesting and fun, especially fun.

For example, award points based on a contact record's completeness. If a record has 10 fields and only four are required, award points for completing the remaining six. Publishing a league table of average scores grouped by owner allows users to measure their own data against that of their colleagues. Rewarding the star performers and champions of good record capture with prizes and recognition creates further engagement and awareness for data quality.

Maintaining data quality is paramount to drive ongoing efficiency in your organization, and these strategies will help you reap the benefits of clean data.

DATA SILOS/DEMOCRATIZATION

Data used to be concentrated in the hands of a few analysts. If you wanted a report pulled, you had to go through at least one person, if not a series of people, to get the information you needed. They had the required codes and keys. Then, if it needed to be tweaked based on feedback, you had to go through that same process all over again.

Today, data should be accessible by any member of any team, but if you don't have the structures, policies, and practices in place to take advantage of it, the information will remain stuck in silos. Cross-collaboration is imperative to take full advantage of data, so you have to break down the silos to achieve its maximum potential.

This is where the democratization of data comes into play. The democratization of data has been a hot topic for a while—and it's finally here for real thanks to the cloud. Business intelligence (BI) no longer rests solely in the hands (and minds) of IT and database administrators. Today all end users, from salespeople to marketers, can have easy access to data and the tools that improve their daily decision making. Cloud BI tools promise an unprecedented level of self-sufficiency to more or less an entire organization.

The promise of easy access to data is certainly achievable today. However, despite the democratization of BI, many organizations have yet to realize the benefits. Organizations are not leveraging BI tools to unlock the easy access to data that is technically very possible. In fact, Gartner surveys reveal that 70 percent of potential BI users in an organization fail to adopt CIO-sponsored analytics tools.[3] With 71 percent of companies planning to increase their analytics budgets in 2016, it is imperative that users adopt new analytics tools and make sure that investment doesn't go to waste.

If you're not ready to implement cloud BI tools like Salesforce Wave Analytics across your entire organization, at least consider a proof-of-concept trial to prove value. Democratization of data is a result of tools and capabilities that, due to the masking of the previous complexity, are incredibly flexible and readily available. Many even use natural language, not code. Organizations are no longer locked into massive requirements gathering before undertaking an analytics project—cloud BI tools allow you to conduct proof-of-concepts with your own data and just a few plug-and-play BI tools. Looking for predictive capabilities? Buy an app. Need an extract, transform, and load (ETL) tool for data migration? Just plug it into your existing CRM. From data enrichment to report creation and data visualization, third-party apps and tools will allow you to empower your teams with self-service BI tools now.

Probably the best example of the democratization of data and its corresponding analytics is IBM's Watson. Remember Watson, the natural language intelligent computer that beat the best human champions of *Jeopardy*? Back then, Watson was physically large (two huge IBM Power Systems racks loaded with encyclopedias of data). Today, Watson is packaged as a cloud service. You can feed it your data, ask it questions in normal language, and watch it pull correlations and insights you didn't think were there, seemingly right before your eyes. You'll scratch your head saying "How the hell could we have missed that?" But you did. It's easy to miss the great gems hidden in your data.

Behind Watson is cognitive science. You communicate with Watson in human language, not code, and it figures out what you are talking about and puts your question or statement into the correct context. A little scary, huh?

IBM has also made Watson almost idiot proof. It's delivered as a cloud-based service. You upload your data and start asking Watson questions in plain English, and Watson will get back to you with correct answers in plain English. If your data isn't sufficient, Watson has access to volumes of information it can tap to enrich your own data. You don't need to own powerful servers, you don't need to build massive databases, code queries that resemble rocket science, or hire armies of PhDs. Watson knows what to do and will walk you through what you need to do as it delivers insights culled from your data.

In short, you use Watson as you would any service in the cloud. IBM is even offering Watson for free to those who want to sample the capabilities for real. These are the real services and you'll get Watson's best shot. When you want to use it seriously with production volumes of data, then you'll pay. But even then, you only pay for what you use. You can, in effect, buy Watson's services by the drink. These paying users can analyze higher volumes of data and tap more data sources, including live links to sources such as data warehouses and cloud sources. Watson is amazing, but don't take my word for it; go to YouTube and watch Watson take on the best human *Jeopardy* champions and win convincingly. And that was Watson several years ago; since then, IBM has enhanced Watson in so many ways that what you encounter in the IBM Watson cloud is light years beyond that initial machine.

WHAT YOU CAN DO NOW

While data democratization may seem like a tall order, it will be a key differentiator for organizations moving forward. When you begin to plan how your organization will make data more accessible, consider how the following criteria could (and should) come into play:

Make data-driven decisions become the norm for end users and their processes. Data should be so abundant across your organization and embedded in business processes that consumption is easy and automatic. Think specifically about how business intelligence (BI) tools can revamp mobile through embedded analytics, rich visualizations, and data-driven workflow integration for your company.

Encourage and enable end users to directly influence how data is presented and consumed. If it's easy for them, they'll adopt the tools. If not, your organization will most likely struggle with poor adoption. But there is no reason it shouldn't be straightforward and easy. The tools are out there.

Align your data visualizations to the organization's key business outcomes. BI tools today are so powerful that they're able to make large data sets immaterial. Only the most relevant information is served up at a given juncture in the workflow process, despite capturing every meaningful customer touch point, relevant structured or unstructured attribute, or new data source like the Internet of Things (IoT). Invest in the art of dashboarding to serve up key metrics that address issues and prompt a next step.

Dashboarding represents an effort to make your data as intuitively clear as the information displayed on the dashboard of your car. You don't want to puzzle over how much gas is in your car. You want to know at a glance when your gas is running low and how far to empty. Same with the temperature gauge; dashboarding tries to clarify complex data and present it in such a way that any manager can get to the point fast.

At Bluewolf we worked with GoodData to come up with an approach to dashboard creation in five simple steps[4]:

1. Understand what attribute dimensions are most appropriate for your business or role, and which chart types will best visualize those dimensions.
2. The best charts show comparative data. This can be historical, year over year, month over month, groupings, or date progressions.
3. Dashboards should be organized so that trends and key performance indicators (KPIs) stand out and are easily identifiable. (The top left chart is usually the chart most people look at first in countries where written languages are left to right.) Also, think about what charts will be seen when the dashboard is first clicked on. The most important charts should be seen in that first screen.
4. Too many colors in a chart will be overwhelming to the reader and will obscure the message. Try another grouping instead. Keep background colors to a minimum.
5. Titles should be descriptive and any assumptions clearly explained. Attribute filters, such as date ranges or territories, should be applied at the dashboard level rather than individual report level whenever possible.

Data can be misleading, and you don't want to be led to the wrong conclusions. Proper visualization of data insights can be just as important as the data itself.

Enable your business with self-service data preparation, data enrichment, and data integration capabilities. Yes, there will be a learning curve and even some resistance (until your employees start seeing what their peers are achieving by way of data preparation). Consider who the users are and what they want out of BI, then develop training for them that will improve adoption. Also, don't forget gamification, one of my favorite strategies for cajoling cooperation and participation. Some modest gamification may be all it takes to get many of your employees to take the data plunge themselves.

IT and the business need to develop partnerships to make this new comingling of capabilities run more smoothly. Business needs to look to IT for insights surrounding data governance and security, while IT needs to be more involved in the business's strategic goals and understand users' needs for data visibility. The path toward data democratization can be disruptive, and for many there may be a turbulent road ahead, but the impact it will have on business outcomes like revenue growth, efficiency, and customer retention will be well worth the investment.

Data management and particularly data governance have become important with the emergence of cloud computing as a primary way organizations work. According to our annual report, *The State of Salesforce*, 64 percent of companies are now releasing new functionality to their Salesforce users at least monthly, up 20 percent from the previous year (Figure 9.1). Companies can achieve this speed of innovation through cloud

Figure 9.1 The State of Salesforce 2015–2016

governance—brief commercial break—especially our Cloud Governance practice, which focuses on building policies, creating governance boards, and deploying application life-cycle technology to fuel ongoing innovation. Unlike traditional governance practices, our approach to cloud governance is specifically intended to align IT and executive strategies, drive short development cycles, and engage the user.

Finally, a last word on master data management and the Salesforce Wave. Let's start with master data management (MDM), a strategy, structure, and practice for managing all data across an organization. Its goal is to ensure that all data in the organization is accurate and consistent, or to put it another way, that there is just one version of the truth. That's a big part of the Bluewolf Customer Covenant from the previous chapter. MDM ensures that every person who interacts with the customer has the same data, and that it is current and accurate.

This is not easy to do. In many cases, a company might have data in different forms, in different systems, for different purposes, all concerning the same customer. This data represents the details and history of the customer relationship, products the customer has purchased, all billing and invoices for the customer, and, to add a little complexity, the vendors used to service a customer or your customer's customers. As if that wasn't complicated enough, your enterprise might have several different business units with different product lines, each with its own departments and its own relationships to the same customers. And it gets worse; some customers use a middle initial with their name, but not necessarily all the time. So, are Joe Smith and Joe M. Smith the same customer or not? Confused yet? In short, MDM recognizes data inconsistencies across customers, multiple departments and systems, and more. It knows that Joe M. Smith is the same Joe Smith whether it is accounting, support, or sales.

This takes us to Wave. Seventy-six percent of companies still struggle with data integration and quality (Figure 9.2), but

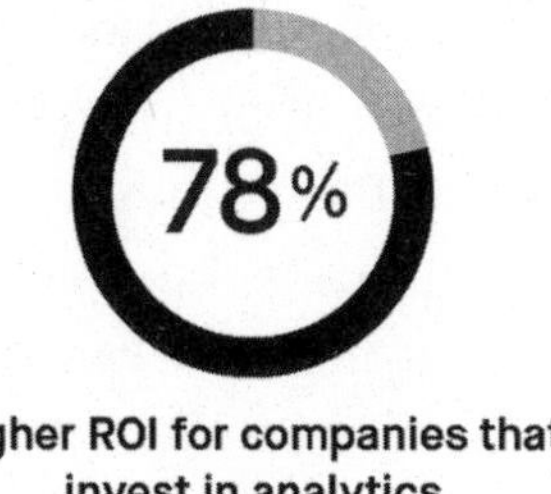

Figure 9.2 The State of Salesforce 2015–2016

Salesforce Wave (or Salesforce Analytics Cloud) promises to change that. MDM really gets critical when you start to apply analytics to the data, which the majority of companies are planning to do. When you do that, you have to be confident that your data is good, meaning consistent, accurate, and current. Ever heard the acronym GIGO (garbage in, garbage out)? Even a little garbage data will pollute or, more accurately, poison your best analytics effort. Suddenly your people cannot be confident in the analytical results. And they are going to be relying on these results to make better business decisions? They might just as well as be wagering on a hunch. If you're struggling with unclean or siloed data, you must understand this problem and fix it.

While I've used Salesforce as my primary example for analytics and statistical measurements, these ideas and concepts can be applied to any cloud-based analytics tools, so don't feel constrained if you are currently using a different CRM platform.

MOBILE AND IOT

You can't think about data, data quality, and master data management without thinking about mobile and, at some point soon, about the IoT. Study after study points to mobile emerging as the dominant way people will access, use, and generate information and initiate transactions now and going forward.

Like the PC was 25 years ago and the laptop 15 years ago, the mobile device is the vehicle all of us will use to access and work with information. Of course, it will be combined with and enhanced by cloud computing, but the mobile device will be dominant. You will use it to get a can of soda from a vending machine; to conduct a transaction with your bank, whether checking your balance or closing a commercial loan; book travel; watch a movie; consult with a doctor; or anything else. We will conduct our lives through the mobile device. In fact, many people already do. That means your business systems have to deal with mobile as a primary input-output device. It will be your wallet, calendar, organizer, address book, house keys, car keys, identification—it will become everything you carry in your pocket, purse, and various satchels (but without the Kleenex).

Now, try this: use your smartphone to access Watson in the IBM cloud and ask it some questions relevant to your business. Go ahead and try it; I'll wait. Back? You're now talking to the future.

Wave is not Watson (nothing except Watson is Watson). Wave now focuses entirely on mobile innovation with features designed specifically for smartphones that allow users to access, integrate, and visualize data generated by Salesforce and partner applications. There is a clearly documented ROI for analytics. In a 2015 interview with *CRM Magazine*, Stephanie Buscemi, Salesforce's senior vice president of analytics, cited two studies that show the growing influence of analytics and mobile, where IDC found a 78 percent higher ROI for companies that invest in analytics and another subsequent study found that 60 percent of online activity now comes from mobile devices.[5] Wave Mobile Connector allows Salesforce customers to start exploring analytics from their phone by importing raw data and transforming it into visual charts or graphs. You can also use Wave Mobile Dashboard Designer to build multifaceted dashboards for visualizing dynamic information from multiple sources. Just follow the five steps mentioned earlier in the chapter.

In short, Adam Bataran, senior director of analytics for Bluewolf, believes the new mobile tools that can be used from any device are able to unleash our clients' data and increase customer intimacy. He further observed that analytics enables companies to know their customers and to make every customer interaction relevant, engaging, and personal. In the end, success with analytics is contingent upon capturing the right data at the right moment and transforming it into valuable insights that improve employees' actions both across an organization and with customers. That has always been the case and I have long harped on that; now it is just a lot easier to do.

Coming back to our discussion about the current onslaught of data, the IoT is ramping up fast. This is where smart devices communicate with other devices, servers, platforms, and whatever else you can think of. The device can be a smartphone or any variety of sensor, appliance, or electronic device with enough intelligence to communicate over an Internet protocol (IP) network. As adoption grows, it will generate enough data to drown you, if you are not drowning in data already. In fact, it can generate so much data that human staff will not be able to keep up. Instead, automation will be required and predictive analytics will steer staff to what is important and needs to be acted on. Remote management and monitoring, alone or combined with predictive analytics, have already emerged as the initial big payback use cases. This is an area that is just emerging, and already the valuations being projected for it—well into the trillions and tens of trillions of dollars—are staggering. Once things can talk to other things, especially over the cloud, almost anything is possible.

For example, what if your product could tell you how your customers were actually using it? Not only marketing folks, but product design and development teams could use this insight to design better, more useful products, products that would work the way customers actually used them. What if your product could automatically call technical support when it sensed a likely failure? It wouldn't take much for intelligent connected systems to connect the dots and have a replacement part ordered, schedule a technician to arrive when the ordered part does, and alert the customer every step of the way. IoT has the potential to change our world in ways we can barely begin to imagine: new ways to go to market, new business models, new capabilities intended to attract completely new market segments, and segments never previously addressed.

Iron Mountain Experience

Using Bluewolf's Actionable Analytics model, Bluewolf helped Iron Mountain build a successful customer retention program using predictive and prescriptive analytics.

Iron Mountain Incorporated, the global leader in storage and information management services, helps more than 220,000 organizations in 45 countries lower storage costs, comply with regulations, recover from disaster, and better use their information, protecting and preserving what matters most.

As part of a global initiative to help improve the customer experience, Iron Mountain turned to Bluewolf three years ago with the goal of reducing customer attrition while increasing renewal rates. By incorporating predictive data models, Iron Mountain was able to increase customer engagement and drive top line growth. As a result:

- Account managers now have the data to successfully manage customer relationships for revenue and retention.
- Analytics has empowered employees to make better decisions, improve processes, and achieve desired outcomes.
- The company overall now defines success as equipping each person to act based on valuable insights delivered by its predictive models.

Furthermore, by leveraging Bluewolf's Actionable Analytics model, Iron Mountain found it could move from the cumbersome data silos of the past to the point where it could achieve specific business outcomes. Better still, the company has since built a customer retention program using predictive and prescriptive analytics, moving storage losses to historic lows.

Bluewolf helped bring Iron Mountain's customer attrition risk analytics into Salesforce, which warns sales reps of attrition risk and prompts action. From past data, Iron Mountain and Bluewolf identified attrition patterns that serve as a series of warning flags. If a customer experiencing a certain set of service issues resembles one of the models, a notification is sent to the correct team so they can proactively correct it.

Finally, through Salesforce, Iron Mountain has the data and advanced reporting to enable its top sales managers to measure their businesses and strategically map out their next best move to manage customer relationships. Iron Mountain proves how sales leaders can apply the lessons of good data and predictive analytics to produce the kind of outcomes that deliver bottom-line value and improve the customer experience.

EXECUTIVE ACTION

With the widespread availability of more and better data combined with easy analytics, we should anticipate what many describe as the arrival of a "new age" in almost religious terms. Overall, most executives will welcome the availability of data and analytics. Some will want to use this data to test new ideas and strategies and conceive new products and services. Heck, the data itself, particularly IoT data, might morph into a new value-added service. Would customers want to know how their people were or weren't using certain products and services, and would they pay a small fee for that insight? Maybe; at this point I don't know, but it's an exciting possibility.

However, those who continue to insist that their gut instincts are always right might not be so happy, especially when those gut decisions are contradicted by the data or proved wrong in practice. If they can't outright avoid data-based decision making, they will play dumb, make excuses, or ignore issues that may upset their gut. Sorry—keep a big bottle of Tums where it can be easily accessed.

Even scarier for this kind of manager will be the realization that there will be few or no places to hide and fewer excuses for wrong decisions or poor performance. There will be incontrovertible data that managers will have to explain, and results for which they will have to hold their teams and themselves accountable. Change is hard, and the arrival of highly accessible data with easy tools to access and understand it will be difficult for some old-school managers. The tools are so easy, however, that data shouldn't be hard to adopt. With Watson available as a free cloud service, there should be no excuse not to at least try data-based decision making.

For most modern managers the arrival of data-based decision making will be welcome, and it will benefit all, whether everyone acknowledges it or not. For example:

- CMOs can use data for nurturing along prospects not quite ready to buy or for leveraging data around more active prospects and customers to cultivate emotional connections with the company brand, product, and services.
- Heads of sales can use data to measure the effectiveness of the selling organization, its productivity, win/loss ratio, pipeline, quality of pipeline, and individual sales performance. In fact, they can show sales reps how to use particular

data nuggets to help close a sale or upsell and cross-sell an existing customer.

- Product development can use the data to better understand what customers want, what they actually use, and how they use the products and services. That can't help but lead to better, more appealing products.
- C-suite executives should use the data to make sharper decisions, identify new areas of opportunity, and address C-level concerns like security and privacy, liability and risk.

In short, there is no area of the modern enterprise that can't benefit from a data-based approach. Facilities management, human resources, tech support—every aspect can be optimized in any number of ways. It's just a question of collecting the appropriate data and looking at it from a fresh perspective, which is what we have analytics for.

It all comes down to the democratization of data. Data is no longer a rare, precious commodity that must be rationed. Today, we have so much data we can drown in it if we aren't careful. Nor can we use it up or need to fear running out. Data is a valuable asset that continually renews itself. The more we share our data assets with the people who work with us and can take advantage of it, the richer we become. They will take that data to enhance the customer experience, employee experience, or partner experience, and the organization will be better off.

Data is never ending. Ninety percent of the world's data has been created in the past two years, and its growth isn't slowing down—the global economy creates 2.5 quintillion bytes of data each day! (FYI, a quintillion=1 followed by 18 zeros) Not only is this massive amount of data collected but it can be analyzed by employees in any department, whether it's sales, marketing, or leadership.

This is the democratization of data, and it will have a profound impact on the business, especially the office culture and specifically on office politics. Yet why aren't more businesses decisions driven by data?

Many organizations today are blind to metrics around cost, high-margin products, and employee productivity. They either don't measure it, or the data is collected and then buried in finance departments. When teams get together for budget or strategy sessions without that data in real time, conversations often devolve into conflict, sometimes described as dueling spreadsheets with conflicting numbers. Rather than focusing on what's objectively best for the business, politics dominates those discussions. I guess many just prefer to trust their gut.

On-demand access to market and internal data can add a layer of extreme objectivity to negotiations and strategic planning. With analytics tools like Salesforce Analytics Cloud or Watson, a team's decisions won't depend upon the loudest or seemingly most authoritative voice. The most persuasive arguments will be supported by clear, clean-cut numbers—without them, your points won't pass muster.

However, don't be naive; presenting this objective data won't automatically drive consensus or bring nirvana. Each executive has a level of accountability around their data. Each member of your team may interpret the data differently or apply it to another scenario. Not everyone will agree, nor should they. Data insights shouldn't replace debate and discussion in decision making, but instead enhance their effectiveness.

For that reason, invest in analytics to get closer to your customers than ever. In the next five years, we'll continue to see refinements and expansions of current analytics technology. Take the next step beyond just collecting data. Leave highly charged office politics behind and make informed, data-based business decisions to provide more value for your customers and your business.

As soon as you finish this chapter, start jotting down the problems you are wrestling with right now and what information would help you solve that problem if only you had it at your fingertips. Ironically, that information probably is sitting in your organization. It might be buried with some other information or need a little organization to make it apparent, but rest assured it is there and closer than you thought. Just look for it. And when you find it, remember: your data and analytics goals need to be driven by business outcomes, not the other way around. If you can't clearly define what it is you need from your data, then restate your need differently, dig deeper for the information, or design a system to provide it. All of the data in the world won't help you provide a better customer experience until you start asking the right questions or pose those questions in the right way. But when you do, you'll be amazed at how much better the customer experience and your business will be.

10

How Good Design Creates Seamless Experiences

A chapter on design! Eric, what were you thinking?

Wait, wait, let me explain. No, I won't ask you to take out crayons and paper and start redesigning the world or even those parts that are particularly important to you. Rather, after going through the practical steps involved in understanding and creating a customer-obsessed culture, this chapter will explain the benefits of integrating that culture with your technical processes, while maintaining flexibility and a great user experience. This entails design thinking at some level and, to be effective, good design. So no, I don't expect readers of this book to stop and pull out their tools and start creating the next-level tablet. But you should cultivate a familiarity with the language of design and build awareness of its basic principles—enough that you can recognize them in action—to appreciate effective and good design. I will provide examples of how tech and great design have enhanced successful companies' focus on people, underscoring the winning message of putting employees and customers first to elevate the customer experience.

Let's start with Nir Eyal's book *Hooked*, which I described in some detail earlier. Eyal was trying to explain why some products capture widespread attention while others flop, a question anyone in business would want to answer. More important, he wants to know what makes us engage with certain products out of sheer habit. He asks whether there is a pattern how technologies hook us. If you go back to Chapter 2, you'll see *Hooked* and Eyal's four-step process described in a bit more detail. In addition to Eyal's analysis, it is really important to think of the impact of poor design.

Most of you reading this book are responsible for driving adoption of some corporate system. Maybe it is Salesforce. And we all know that Salesforce is possibly the easiest tool on the planet to add features and functionality, which generally come in the form of fields, workflows, picklists, and reports. Now, peer into your personal life. Which applications do you use on your phone, tablet, or laptop? Do you *welcome* more fields, workflows, or reports? Quite the opposite. The consumer world is teaching us that good design *gets rid* of these things. At the surface level, good design does more, but with less. Good design is why Apple, Amazon, and Uber are extraordinarily valuable companies.

As important, bad design is what abandons the end user. Bad design is the number one thing that will assure your initiative will fail, no matter how critical it may be. Furthermore, bad design is what will create ill will with your end users (employees) or customers, and what will decrease their engagement with your brand. And disengaged employees wreak havoc on your culture, and disengaged customers are, well, not customers at all. That's the impact.

So what exactly is good design and good design thinking? Before we dive into the nitty gritty, let's take a quick look at a real-world example. TurboTax, an online tax-filing platform, specializes in making the annual filing process as easy as possible. Their customers range from having simple to mildly complicated tax returns that shouldn't need additional review from a CPA, which can cost quite a bit of money. TurboTax recognized that one of the most arduous parts of the process is entering financial data. To solve this pain point, they designed a picture to populate W-2 function—just snap a photo of your W-2, upload it to their system, and watch the little cells instantly fill themselves. Their focus wasn't just on the end goal (tax filing), but on the entire user experience. To elevate the customer experience, it's no longer enough to just solve a problem—you have to start thinking like a designer and improve every step and interaction along the way.

DESIGN

Design has been a part of human existence since time immemorial. From the earliest design and development of primitive tools to illuminated manuscripts to industrial design in the nineteenth century and beyond, design has played an integral function in our society, and it continues to do so today. On a day-to-day basis, most of us don't consider the design that shapes how we experience the world. We might notice and appreciate the artistry, good taste, and ease of use of an object. However, it is rare for the average person to stop and analyze the design decisions that molded that experience. Good design, and the resulting good experience, is simply there. We only really notice it when it's lacking or, to be fair, particularly stunning.

Bluewolf is headquartered in New York City, where amazing design can be experienced almost everywhere you turn. One that repeatedly surprises me is the brilliance of Central Park (Figure 10.1). That someone decided to carve out a huge chunk in the center of what was already emerging as a dense city and then preserve it forever as a natural area is astonishing. Given the huge demands the public puts on it, Central Park's versatility and flexibility is incredible. Everyone who has ever been to Central

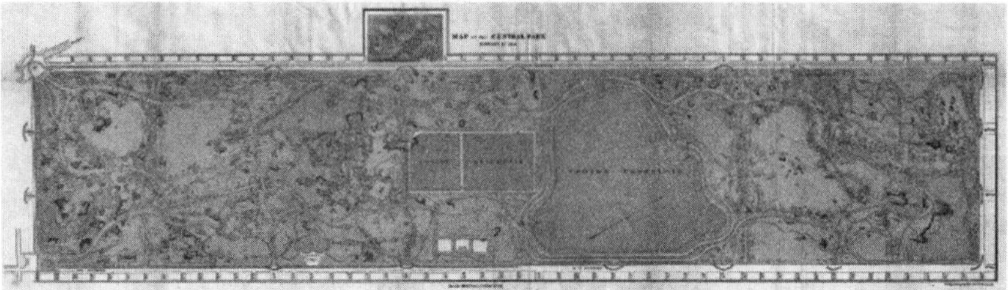

Figure 10.1 Central Park Map, 1860[1]

Park has their favorite spot, their own niche, and it's different for each person you ask. Let's make this a hallmark of good design: One way or another, a person's experience with good design is always a pleasant one. The point that is often forgotten is that Central Park didn't just happen. It was deliberately orchestrated. It was dreamt up and created by Frederick Law Olmsted and Calvert Vaux, each of whom went on to become a world-renowned landscape designer. In a bustling city of over, at the time, one million people, they wanted to create an artistic, aesthetically pleasing refuge that mimicked those found in the countryside and in England. To that end, you'll find many dirt paths and secluded areas, as well as large open fields for sports, picnics, and other social activities. My personal favorites are Sheep Meadow, the Shakespeare Garden, and the dirt path through the North Woods.

When I talk about design, I'm not only talking about visual, graphic, or environmental design, which is what most people probably think of first. Visual design is important, but there is another aspect of design, user experience (UX) design, that has a huge impact on customer experience. UX design addresses the functional or practical aspects of a product, rather than just how it looks. Is it easy to use? Fun? Useful? All of those are considerations of UX design.

In practical terms, design is your engagement hook. Customers want a frictionless experience—wherever, whenever. One way you can do this is to reduce the data to the customer moment. In other words, use design to filter the data into something useful for your customers. Think of the suggestions ribbon at the bottom of every page on Amazon. It automatically repopulates based on your search history and what you're browsing right at that moment. Good design serves as the bridge between data and culture/engagement. It hooks users in, driving adoption without taking them out of the moment.

In any good design, the visual and functional aspects must blend in a balanced and effective way for successful results. I'm not talking about the avant-garde; I'm talking about the everyday realities of the average person walking down the street who has 15 minutes to get to a meeting, is trying to decide between the subway or a cab, while simultaneously jotting down last-minute notes on the way there. What do they need from your design and their technology or the things they are carrying with them to ensure the best experience for them under these particular circumstances?

That's all a big part of design, too. Lately, especially since the iPhone arrived, we call this the user experience (UX), and the visual component connecting the user with the backend tech is the user interface (UI). Under Steve Jobs's watchful eye, Apple's UI and UX designers nailed that first iPhone experience and have been refining it ever since. They did it not by making it pretty, but by making it intuitive.

Even for products like the iPhone, however, design alone isn't enough to get you to buy one. You don't buy something because everyone is buying it. Fads like that die out within a few months, leaving thousands of dissatisfied users in their wake. You buy it because it will enable you or solve a problem. So the first question you have to answer is how does the product or service help you? If you can't explain why you need it and how it improves your life, then you don't really need it no matter how intuitive or beautiful it is, or how slick the UI/UX may be.

This is not to say that the UX isn't important. On the contrary, the UX is the result of a very deliberate and methodical process that aims to understand the users and predict what they want or need before they know it themselves. It involves the detailed observation and analysis of user behavior to predict their next actions and needs. Let me leave it to the UX experts at Bluewolf to explain further using the handy graphic in Figure 10.2.

There is a misconception about UI/UX that can lead you astray. Too often, people assume UI/UX design is merely a supplementary feature to attract clients, peers, and colleagues; some sparkling bling to drape around your product. Thinking of

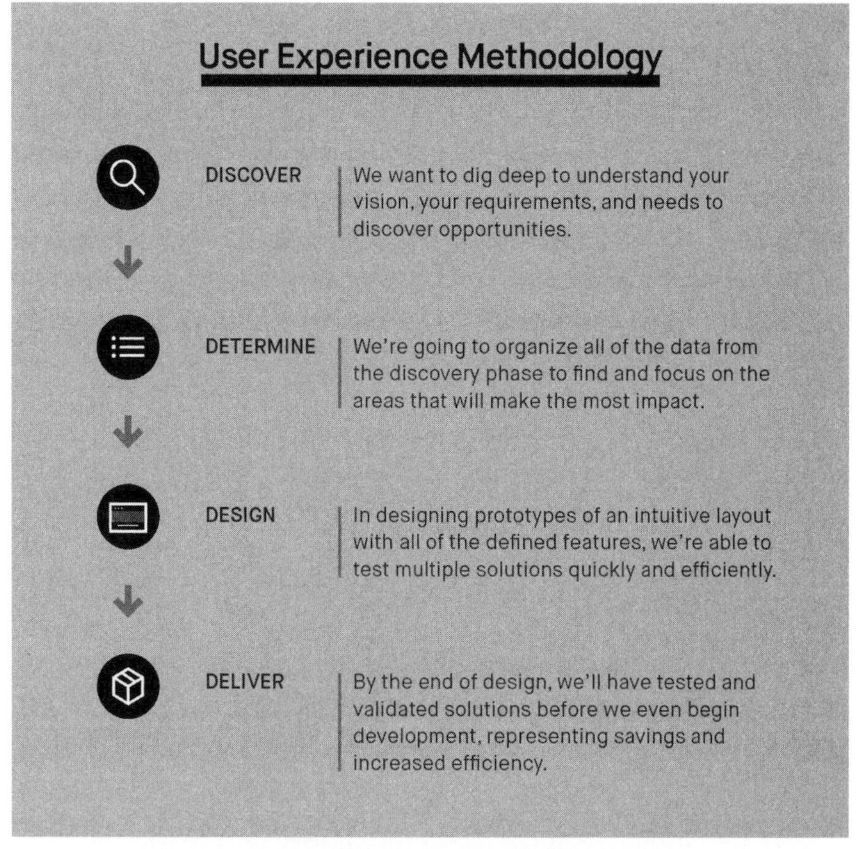

Figure 10.2 ***The State of Salesforce*** **2015–2016**

UI/UX as a secondary need, however, can be a fatal flaw. Designing an outstanding UI/UX should be viewed as an organization-wide effort bent on capturing the best vision of what your customers or users need and want, and who may not even be able to clearly articulate it. You will have to surmise what they don't say based on your analysis of what your customers actually do with the product: when and where they use it, how often, and every other data point you can think of that will give you insight into what they want next. This is not easy. At Bluewolf, we go through about a dozen different steps in designing the right UX for a client. UX isn't just the look and feel of the product, it is the way you encapsulate how the product and process actually works.

Let's sum up the design effort in three statements: (1) Design is just one part of the larger process; (2) the design process, especially UX design, takes time and a significant investment; and (3) as with everything else I'm writing about, listen to the data. That listening is what, in the end, requires the most time and effort. Every single customer-focused company that is serious about remaining competitive invests in design. Don't believe me? Take a look at two of the hottest companies in travel today.

AIRBNB

Airbnb's rental model solves an obvious problem for both the traveler and the property owner, but beyond that, their website offers an impressive user experience. It's easy to navigate, offers customizable experiences based on your location, and splits its offerings into different categories as you scroll through: "explore the world," "weekend getaway," and so on. They even offer an "instant book" button for users who want to guarantee their stay immediately. Lastly, their brand showcases photos to create an anticipatory experience; you feel as though you are coming home even before you arrive.

(*continued*)

(*continued*)
Virgin America

Virgin disrupted the airline industry by establishing itself as a design-led brand that shifted the focus of the flying experience to its customers. When Virgin entered the market eight years ago, other airlines were squeezing in more seats and adding on fees to cope with higher operating costs, while Virgin's number one priority was the customer. From more legroom to a rewards program with perks for even the average, infrequent flyer to a fun flying experience that begins with a music video that doubles as a safety announcement, they have always been ahead of the curve.

Virgin and Airbnb are successful because their obsession with user experience shifted their lens and connected them to their audience. It's never been about what's right for them, but about what's right for their customers. They dug into customer pain points in the hotel and airline industries and figured out how to deliver not just a different experience but a more delightful one.

SIMPLICITY

A few years ago, John Maeda wrote a book called *The Laws of Simplicity*, in which he identified 10 laws that you can use to simplify your life. He categorizes them into topics like design, business, technology, and life. Over the past few years, design, business, and technology have undergone a dramatic change, but his rules still apply. As for life, it remains chaotic, so his laws are needed as much as ever before.

Let's take a look at the first and last of Maeda's laws. The first, Reduce, promises that "the simplest way to achieve simplicity is through thoughtful reduction."[2] Which elements can be removed with either no difference or improvements made to the user experience? The final law, which he calls The One, says simplicity is about "subtracting the obvious and adding the meaningful."[3] Amen to that.

One of Bluewolf's clients, a national post office (anonymized for privacy), presents an interesting case in reducing complexity to deliver a better experience. They have been keeping their citizens connected for more than 200 years by delivering mail, helping businesses and consumers with parcels, and providing a national retail network that supports local communities and organizations. As the needs of the community have evolved, so has the organization, with a range of services spanning its stores, both online and at digital mailboxes. It has unrivaled community-based post office and delivery networks that underpin connection and commerce for all citizens.

The postal service wanted to solve a series of common business issues that were affecting the customer and employee experiences. Like many organizations, employees had to enter data into multiple systems, sales and marketing weren't aligned to serve the customer, and data and customer touch points were slipping through the cracks. This is in stark contrast to what they are known for—establishing and maintaining personal relationships on the front line through retail stores and parcels/letters delivery—and they wanted to return to achieving their high standards on a consistent basis across the country.

The company's search for a solution led them to Bluewolf. We helped them implement Service Cloud, a single platform for all of their agents to use. The platform enables case management, automated workflows, queue routing and reporting, and dashboards. Additionally, Bluewolf helped them to deploy computer telephony integration to capture information from the phone system to identify customers and collect information from back-end systems before customer service receives a call. We also integrated the postal service's back-end systems for parcel information, ServiceNow, Portals, SMS, and Marketing Cloud.

Lastly, we assisted in the development of consumer and customer portals and developed a simplified inquiry process.

The results could not have been better. The new system resolved the systems and data problems, streamlined their workflow, and improved business efficiency. Specifically, it allowed the organization to:

- Reduce the number of clicks for a typical "Where's my parcel" inquiry from 160 to 11 clicks, bringing it down from nine screens to two;
- Reduce the number of CRM systems from three to one;
- Enable at least 1,000 new registrations for the business portal to date with a large number of customers listing it as their preferred medium of contact; and
- Generate over 100,000 logins to the consumer portal in the first month with a 70 percent revisit rate.

This postal service's primary focus has always been its customers. They just needed an improved UI/UX process and design to keep up with increased demand and new customer expectations.

CONVERGENCE OF DATA, DESIGN, AND CULTURE

Good ideas fail all the time. For ideas to succeed, you have to combine them with data, design, and a culture willing to adopt them. Sounds simple, right? Maybe more like magic; just direct your data, design, and culture to work in concert, sort of like the sorcerer in *The Sorcerer's Apprentice* to achieve growth, engagement, and retention. I wish it were that simple. Without adhering to the right principles and processes, you're more likely to end up like the apprentice, panicking over dancing brooms and mops while the room slowly fills up with water.

Great design can indeed be simple, but it requires data to execute well. If you don't have the right data, you can't accommodate good, prescriptive design. Dive into the data, conduct Rep Rides, and map out the customer journey. Then you can build on the data to feed your customers an incredible, intuitive design that doesn't make them figure out what comes next or wrestle with data architecture. Great design sees the world from the perspective of the customer or end user, not the designer.

Remember when companies collected and stored a finite amount of data about their products, employees, and customers in antiquated internal CRM systems like those from Siebold (now part of Oracle)? That was the age of enterprise resource planning. Now, there is an unlimited amount of data about customers and unlimited amounts of low-cost, highly accessible storage to save it. Consider that both an opportunity and a challenge.

Not surprisingly, people are struggling to manage this deluge of data. According to Bluewolf's *The State of Salesforce* report, 76 percent of Salesforce users struggle with integration and data quality. Additionally, 70 percent of users enter the same data into multiple systems (Figure 10.3). That needs to change. We have unlimited data, but how do we put it effectively into the hands of

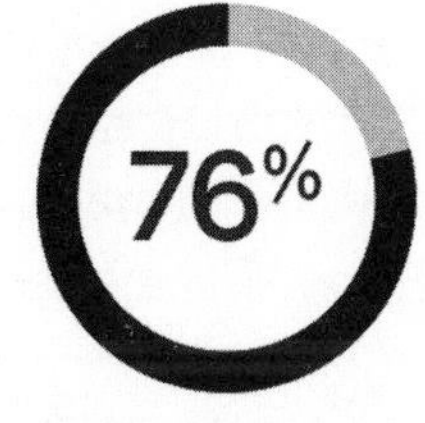

Figure 10.3 ***The State of Salesforce*** **2015–2016**

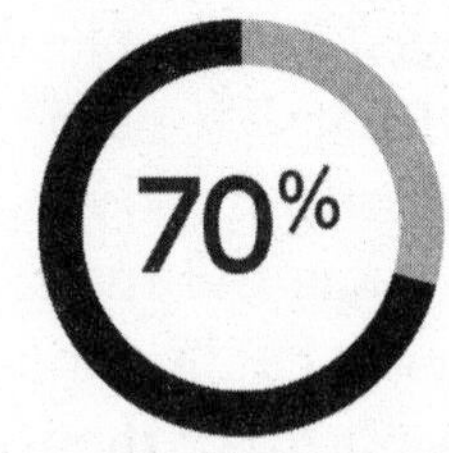

Figure 10.4 ***The State of Salesforce*** **2015–2016**

end users? Live data must be managed through simple, intuitive design, and the best way to accomplish that is by designing for the customer moment.

Great design requires understanding the customer journey and employee realities. You have to learn, not assume. Don't fall into the conference room trap—get out there and experience it for yourself. That's what the Rep Rides you've heard me talk about do; they let you experience what your customer experiences.

Rep Rides are Bluewolf's term for standing in the customer's shoes or, more likely, sitting next to the customer as you go on a sales call together. It is mainly about trying to experience the customer's day-to-day realities (and problems) as closely as you can. It is our version of a day-in-the-life exercise. You can then share the captured data with your user experience/user interface (UX/UI) team and use it to design a better experience.

A few months ago, a Bluewolf team spent two days observing a leading media outlet's customer service reps in inbound and outbound capacities as they performed their work-related activities. During the time spent with each person, the Bluewolf team member asked a series of questions designed to understand business needs while also closely observing current behaviors. It is not unusual for someone to say one thing and do something else. Anyone who has children must be familiar with this. In this case, the experience was being built around Salesforce and the team was looking for potential gaps between the Salesforce system's known interactions and what the company's employees were actually doing.

Our Rep Ride team discovered that 59 percent of employees reported pain points directly related to issues with Salesforce usage. However, 80 percent reported wanting fewer Salesforce screens (also known as pages). In short, they wanted more efficiency and access to more information, but in a much more concise format. How to do that was left to our design team.

In another finding, employees felt that decreased handling time was key to their success. They believed their efficiency was hampered by the complexity of their system and that their conversion rate would increase if they had more bundle options (packages) to offer. Basically, they thought that Salesforce was giving them too many options that had to be explained. Instead, they wanted bundled options that combined different features. This again was a design challenge once we uncovered the issue. The design team just had to figure out the combinations of options that proved most popular and put them together.

You read in Chapter 5 about our work with the Bay Club, a San Francisco-based health club, to identify the pain points preventing sales reps from upselling and cross-selling successfully. We even spent time in the field with the reps, observing, asking questions, and recording data to understand their day-to-day

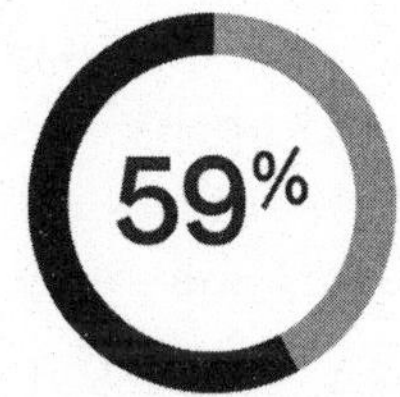

Figure 10.5 ***The State of Salesforce*** **2015–2016**

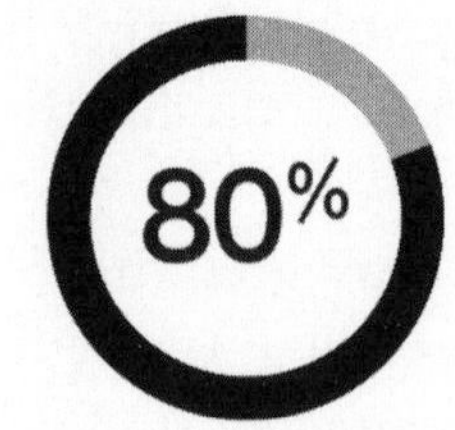

Figure 10.6 ***The State of Salesforce* 2015–2016**

experience. We discovered that in-person touch points, while central to the Bay Club brand, were ineffective in driving additional sales, because the reps couldn't access customer data efficiently. We took those insights and translated them into a mobile app designed to provide live customer data including facility preferences, activity levels, and class participation to increase sales, while maintaining the deep human connection central to Bay Club's philosophy.

Great design doesn't just satisfy a visual requirement; it requires a deep understanding of the goals and experiences of end users. Your employees, once they are properly informed, are the ones best positioned to drive engagement with customers. Their ability to convey your brand's values is 100 percent tied to the strength of your culture and the quality of the information you feed into it. In that sense, your culture can make or break your company's—or any company's—success.

Culture, data, and design work in concert to achieve growth, engagement, and retention. They enable companies to do more with less, faster. That's why we gave this book the title we did. Great design is simple. However, despite all the volumes you see written on big data, the data I'm talking about here isn't big at all; it's small and streamlined.

For example, I encounter a lot of bad design in my travels. Good design, on the other hand, does not need an explanation. Good design is *not* being presented with 500 channels when you turn on a TV in a foreign place when all you are looking for is the NCAA final and have no idea what channel or even what network it might be on. Nobody has the time or patience to click through all those channels. Good design is walking into a room and telling the television "turn on the game" and it does. Impossible? One large cable TV packager is promoting almost exactly that. Clearly, some designer has figured out how to do it.

POWER OF STORYTELLING

Much of what you need to do in creating a great customer or worker experience is to build a user experience that draws them in with a compelling, emotional story. Based on the lesson conveyed in a piece called "How to Design Happiness" by head creatives Randall Stone, Gabby Etrog Cohen, and Bruce Vaughn, who work for Disney, Lippencott, and SoulCycle, the UX will have three major elements: structure of anticipation, experience, and memory.[4]

Anticipation comes first. The anticipation of the experience is sometimes greater than the experience itself. How many pleasurable hours do you spend planning and daydreaming about the details of your next vacation?

Your design also will need to draw in your target audience emotionally. It should bite into your brand narrative, but that's not enough. You want it to illustrate the ways in which your customers can and should be connecting with you, presumably by using your product or service. Just think of how Levi's Stadium, home of the San Francisco 49ers, uses its mobile application to connect with fans. It creates a shared experience from the very beginning stages of the customer journey by guiding you through the ultimate fan experience, complete with mobile snack delivery to your seat.

The end moment should have the biggest impact, as it's the part everyone remembers most clearly. One study cited by the above article found that "waiters who gave mints at the end of the meal received 3 percent higher tips, while those who presented the mints with just a bit more effort, asking the question 'would anyone like mints at the end of their meal?' received 14 percent higher tips. It shows that we're biased to remember endings by nature."[5] And a positive, pleasurable ending is the best of all.

Let me finish this section with a few more thoughts on design: Great design isn't cheap, and it shouldn't be since it can do so much for you. Another point is what I call the modern art conundrum. You know, where a museum displays a piece of modern art—maybe a can of soup nailed onto a board—that sold for, say, $2 million, and some loudmouth says "I could do that!" Yes, he could have, but he didn't, and until he just saw it, he never even would have thought of doing it.

Another reason great design isn't cheap is that it requires extensive research, time, and thought, each of which costs money. Too many companies treat design like the redheaded stepchild, not even bothering to read an introductory book on design principles to understand the impact of good design on customer experience. Then, when those companies hire outside experts, they try to cut corners because they don't have a good understanding of what's important. That's when you buy cheap once and then buy a second time to finally do the job right. If you are a particularly slow learner or dangerously cheap, you could end up buying a third, or even fourth, time.

MOBILE

When did you realize you wanted a smartphone? If you're like most people, it was around the time you realized that a

BlackBerry would allow you to access your e-mail on the go. Initially, smartphones were about a nifty gadget and all the cool things you could do with it away from the office, all the apps and the great user experience. Now, having a smartphone from Apple or any other vendor is about focusing on what people need, what they want, and how often they will use it. When evaluating a mobile application's development, one of the most important things to consider is can it stand alone? Or does it need to be integrated into larger apps? Can those apps even function well on a smartphone or tablet? What about smartwatches?

With the right handful of core apps and some selected cloud functionality, there is almost nothing you cannot do with your smartphone or tablet that you couldn't do back in your office. Actually, depending on the apps and the cloud services you set up, there may be things you can *only* do on your smartphone or tablet. It's ironic that the devices we invented to save time have now blurred the lines between our on/off hours, but we can always look at it as good practice for setting professional boundaries.

Employees say it's easier to do their jobs when they can access work remotely from a mobile device. Their coworkers, customers, and partners would probably agree. Mobile reinvention of the most time-consuming tasks is one of the best ways to improve the employee experience, but it's no longer only about putting an app for everything on your mobile device. It's really about driving higher adoption of tools and customer and employee/partner engagement in the field.

Just a year or two ago, Apple teamed up with IBM with the goal of bringing about 100 enterprise applications to the mobile platform. When that happened, the consensus among the mainframe enthusiasts was that maybe Apple could teach IBM about intuitive design, at least in terms of UI and UX and maybe some of that would filter over to IBM's enterprise platforms themselves.

But IBM is no slouch at design, either; they have IBM iX. This is an IBM group that exists at the intersection of business, art, and technology. Its goal is to understand that to grow in the digital era, businesses need to do more than keep up—they must predict future trends and act on ideas. So IBM iX teams transform brands, grow businesses, and delight customers by identifying opportunities and acting with agility to design innovations that scale for the global economy.

Last year the Apple–IBM joint apps began rolling out, and the reviews have been pretty good. Not sure how many mainframes sales the mobile apps are stimulating, but mobile apps are clearly driving workloads on the mainframe almost through the proverbial roof. Mainframe shops will in many cases pay extra when their workloads surpass a certain level. IBM mainframe customers noticed the surge in billable traffic peaks due to mobile activity. In response, IBM initiated a discount program that lowers the cost of this additional mainframe workload traffic. It turns out that behind every mobile click by someone seeking one or another cloud-based service, such as checking their current bank balance, booking a flight, and doing any number of other transactions from their mobile device—the heavy lifting sits on a mainframe. It is the mainframe that handles these transactions, ensures their security, and enables high availability of what often are very complex compound transactions. This work drives mainframe peak workload charges so much that IBM felt compelled to discount the charges. Without changing the mainframe's basic role, mobile is poised to dramatically alter mainframe traffic/workload patterns. The mainframe will continue as the always available, highly secure and scalable back-end resource that delivers information on request and handles massive volumes of transactions while remaining nearly invisible to most people.

Mobile will also play a big part in the emerging Internet of Things, driving vast exchanges of information. Think wearables, too, which are just another form of the mobile device and more things on the Internet of Things. By the way, wearables, too, will likely drive more mainframe workload on the back end as health and fitness organizations and service providers collect and process what will amount to massive volumes of personal health and fitness info.

Salesforce, too, has had its eye on helping companies engage with their mobile customers. Advances and growth in the Salesforce1 platform as well as the introduction of Salesforce's first mobile apps—Salesforce Classic, Salesforce Touch, Chatter Mobile, and the most recent Salesforce1 mobile app—have all demonstrated leaps forward in delivering the mobile revolution to companies in the Salesforce ecosystem.

According to Bluewolf's 2015 *The State of Salesforce* report, Salesforce1 mobile adoption is exploding. In its first year (2015), 89 percent of Salesforce customers adopted the Salesforce1 mobile application, and its user base is continuing to grow. Additionally, Salesforce1 users are twice as likely to build custom mobile apps.

Among the most difficult aspects of going mobile is designing your application for multiple devices and interfaces. Salesforce aims to simplify and standardize this issue by providing its own set

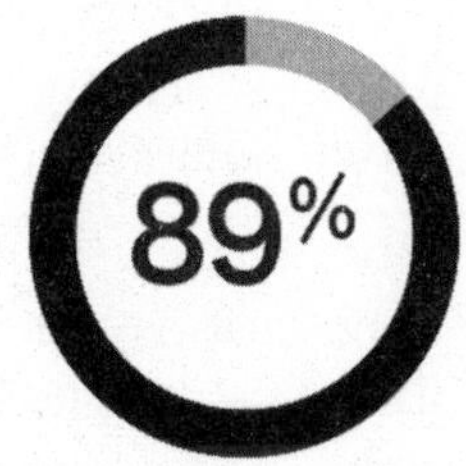

Figure 10.7 ***The State of Salesforce* 2015–2016**

of components for developers when developing apps built on the Salesforce platform. This provides a consistent experience for end users, as well as a consistent appearance to commonly used components in desktop and mobile applications. Additionally, this aids in the overall adoption of the platform, as it provides users with a more intuitive and standardized approach to interacting with their Salesforce instance. Check out the accompanying sidebar for the latest on Salesforce's Lightning tools.

Lightning AppBuilder is a unified development tool that allows a developer to simultaneously develop for all form factors using push-button deployment. This feature allows a developer to create a single application that can be deployed to any device and customized to the specific use case and form factor. According to a recent study commissioned by Facebook, more than 60 percent of online adults use at least two devices every day, while a quarter of online Americans use three devices. These trends make the Lightning AppBuilder particularly advantageous, as multidevice and multibrowser use become the new standard.

Lightning Components are prebuilt functionalities that can be integrated into Salesforce applications using a simple drag-and-drop model. Through the reusable components model, Lighting will enable very rapid iteration of new application features to meet changing customer demands and experience expectations. Additionally, customers can build their own components, buy them on the AppExchange like traditional ISV applications, or work with consulting partners like Bluewolf to have them built.

Lightning Connect combines the External Data Services and External Objects features of the platform, using a new standard called "OData" to dynamically query or retrieve information from back office or legacy apps and databases, and then present it in the context of a Salesforce standard or custom object.

Lightning Process Builder constructs business process flows that lead users through the required steps to execute a business process or transaction. Everything from simple to highly complex processes can be modeled and enforced in the application.

Lightning Community Designer is a rebranding of the Communities Designer tool, used to rapidly create branded public or private communities. At this point, it's unclear as to whether the same components available in the AppBuilder will be available here.

So what does all of this mean for your business? Lightning will enrich customer, employee, and partner interactions by providing a simple, consumer-like interface that delivers fresh, up-to-the-moment data in context. Previously, a lot of build time would go into designing mobile or desktop-friendly interfaces that feed from Salesforce data. With Salesforce Lightning, the design-build-deploy cycle for the majority of business processes and functions has been cut down, thereby allowing developers to release apps and get feedback from end users faster. As today's businesses pivot and change rapidly, this toolset allows a better bedrock for pilot development and proof of concepts, before having to look into developing bespoke applications.

While the release of Salesforce Lighting has made it easier to deploy Salesforce customizations across devices, there are still the same limitations that come with all web-based mobile apps. Mainly, the lack of ability to utilize native hardware functionality, speed, and secure offline access.

For Bluewolf, Lightning expands our ability and is another way to help our customers to optimize their customer moments—all the touch points with customers, be it in person, over the phone, or unmediated customer self-service.

One last word about IBM Watson. When I talk about design being driven by data, I also want to add that it's driven by analytics, too. The data can quantify what's going on, but analytics will tell you what it means. IBM Watson excels at both sorting, filtering, and correlating vast amounts of data, even seemingly confusing data, and then drawing conclusions from the data patterns you never suspected were there, all at lightning speed. Watson's agile, ever-improving artificial intelligence should enable designers to produce better, more customer-focused designs than ever before.

As with every business idea, process, and application, the heart of design—and the intertwining influences of data and company culture—resides in people. The cloud isn't a bubble, and your company's UI/UX has a direct impact on your partners, employees, and customers. How will you make yourselves stand out and reshape the customer experience?

One of my favorite ways of defining that idea and effort is the purple cow. Driving through cow country on a road trip, you get excited when you see a few cows for the first time, but as you get farther in, the sight becomes common and you're more focused on escaping the smell of manure than on noticing the subtle differences between the herds. But imagine if 50 miles in you saw a herd of purple cows. You'd sit up in your seat, stop the car, and grab your camera. That's what you need to capture through great design—the purple cow. For years, Corinne Sklar, Bluewolf's chief marketing officer, has framed the idea of innovation through the purple cow, which means standing out from the sea of sameness that all of your competitors are swimming in. You've likely already invested quite a bit of time and effort into researching your company's customer experience. Now is the time to take it and design a cow in your own, very unique shade of purple.

11

Digital Marketing

Standing Out in the Sea of Sameness

Imagine being a fashion company in the late '80s/early '90s. Global styles and brands are more accessible to the middle class than ever before; your traditional marketing mailers, magazine spreads, and television segments are touching tens of thousands of potential buyers; and your brand is well recognized and trusted as a quality clothing provider.

Now flash forward to today. People can shop the latest trends via their smartphones and compare prices across multiple brands so they can find the best deal. Your brand, established decades ago, has undergone a cultural shift that is depressing sales. This was the exact situation Burberry experienced just a few years ago.

Burberry needed to reinvigorate its brand while improving the connection between the company and its customers. They used targeted social media and digital ad campaigns to transform from an aging icon into a global luxury brand. Their most successful viral marketing campaign was (and is) the "Art of the Trench," a social campaign where customers can share photos of themselves wearing Burberry coats, highlighting their individual styles. This served a dual purpose: brand awareness and peer-to-peer validation and evangelism. Burberry had built a highly regarded and respected brand over generations. It was determined not to let this value evaporate and took advantage of the latest digital marketing technology to reinvent itself.

Business has truly become a digital world. Marketing is no different, and why should it be? Digital marketing has opened up a host of new opportunities for customer connection, but this has also complicated an already challenging and delicate process. We not only have more customer touch points, but the amount of content produced every day by marketers and consumers is staggering. This is generally a positive thing, but it has downsides, too, that must be recognized and addressed. This chapter will explore the changes brought by the advent of digital marketing and discuss the most effective strategies for incorporating digital channels into your marketing and brand strategy to create a better customer experience.

MARKETING: CRASH COURSE

Marketing is not the same as advertising. You could debate endlessly the definitions of marketing and advertising, but that is a fruitless effort and life is too short. Here is a definition of marketing that works for me: Marketing is the process and set of activities for creating, communicating, delivering, and exchanging offers that have value for customers, clients, partners, and society at large. By offers, I don't just mean "Half price through the weekend." *Offer* refers to any attribute of any thing that the marketer enhances and chooses to emphasize as a way of representing value.

At the risk of revealing my age, marketers have long talked about the marketing mix, which represents a collection of product attributes. Classic marketing focuses on the four

Ps of the marketing mix: product, price, promotion, and place (distribution). As a marketer, these are the four classic levers you can work to drive your marketing strategy. Different strategies may emphasize one lever or another. In more recent years the four Ps have been expanded to as many as seven and the P has been replaced by a C. And the variations don't stop there. For the purposes of this book, though, the four Ps work well.

One other distinction I want to make is between traditional and digital marketing. Here the distinction mostly reflects the media represented. Digital implies electronic or computerized. The primary digital channels include: social, website, mobile and mobile apps, search engine optimization (SEO), and e-mail. The list of digital channels continues to grow with the inclusion of virtual reality, augmented reality, and more, including some not fully envisioned yet.

By way of comparison, the traditional channels include radio, television, mail, billboards, and face-to-face (which usually takes the form of a human sales rep, but it can also include an encounter at a trade show, convention, or conference).

One of the advantages of digital channels is that the product and the message are, by definition, digitized. That means they can be read by computers and, under various circumstances, enhanced by them, too.

IMPORTANCE OF BRAND

You can't talk about marketing without talking about brand. A brand is more than just a logo. A brand is typically associated with a specific organization or company and connotes certain attributes, qualities, and capabilities. Marketers can invest enormous amounts of money to create, design, define, establish, promote, and then protect their brand. The best-marketed brands are those that establish an emotional connection with people.

This emotional connection with your brand directly impacts the customer experience. There is a reason people prefer brand name products over the cheaper generic versions. It's this sense of relationship and reputation between the brand and customers that makes it so enormously valuable to the company. Think about the first time you had to buy paper towels for your own apartment. You'd just moved out of your parents' house, you were completely broke, and felt torn between Bounty, the trusted, quicker picker-upper regularly stocked above your childhood home's kitchen sink, and the generic brand that was a few dollars cheaper. Chances are, you pitched the pack of Bounty into your cart and justified it by telling yourself you'd make one less coffee run at work the next week. That's the power of a great brand.

Brands are everywhere and have been for over a century. The Sears catalog was a household brand back in America's pioneer days. Ford was established as a leading auto brand early in the twentieth century. The company that became IBM was founded in 1911 as the Computing-Tabulating-Recording Company. Later it became International Business Machines. And today we know it as IBM. Brand identities can morph into something else, but it is a hard trick to pull off. (Full disclosure: In the spring of 2016 IBM purchased Bluewolf. We're not expecting to change the Bluewolf brand except to the extent it evolves naturally as we tap into IBM's other capabilities as we continue to serve our customers.)

Brand-based marketing predates the digital era by decades. However, digital has fundamentally changed the nature of how people buy. In short, people research the products they are considering to buy extensively before they make their decision. They have read the reviews online. They have seen the product sheets and technical details. They have reviewed competitive analyses. They have seen and heard about the best, most viral products via social media. Your customers are doing so much research prior to a sale that it's imperative to make sure your brand is well known and well represented in the digital marketplace. People don't even have to break a sweat to shop or compare prices on the go. They just type your name and product into Google, and find more than you probably imagine is out there—the good, the bad, and the ugly. It's your job to maximize the good and minimize the bad and ugly. The primary vehicle for this is content related to your brand. Your brand speaks through all content, whether it's produced by your company or someone else. All of that content—company blogs, white papers, reviews, social tags, sentiments of others—has an inordinate impact on brand perceptions.

The trick to succeeding in digital marketing is to establish your voice, have a clear point of view, and then maintain it and protect it. Bluewolf made a point to do that early on, and one of our biggest moves to support that goal has been our annual *The State of Salesforce* report. When we first published the report, Salesforce wasn't enthusiastic. Rather than providing a shining endorsement, we provided an accurate, unflinching analysis of the software-as-a-service (SaaS) market and Salesforce's position within it. We weren't afraid to take control of messaging around cloud and SaaS, despite competing with consulting giants like Deloitte. Call it chutzpah mixed with fearlessness, but the result of this ambition has been huge market influence as our findings are used again and again by industry leaders all over the world. Our efforts with *The State of Salesforce* have inspired numerous spinoffs. Salesforce itself released its first "State of Marketing" report in 2016. What can your company do to differentiate its voice from the competition?

When it comes to brand content, too often marketing departments focus on the final stages of the sales funnel before closing, to the detriment of landing potential clients still in the early inquiry phase. At Bluewolf, our CMO, Corinne Sklar, urges her team to focus not only on the opportunities close to conversion but also the lead time required to turn inquiries into genuine interest. Bluewolf's demand funnel integrates sales and marketing with a pronounced focus on handoff points between the two departments. The funnel attempts to leverage all of the native functionality in the system, which reduces the work the inside sales team would have to do to reinvent content we already had. Finally, our marketing team fine-tunes Bluewolf's return-on-investment strategy since sales for the solution provider are typically complex and involve multiple influencers and points of contact at the end-user company. Bluewolf's model, however, tracks which marketing tactics are touching end users at different points in the sales process and assesses their effectiveness. This allows us to tweak our process to ensure money is being allocated to the activities most likely to generate a return.

Most organizations think the goal of marketing is to convert prospects into customers. That's a good start, but it's not enough. Your goal should be to convert customers into advocates for your brand. Are people tweeting about you, blogging about you, tagging you on Instagram, and Snapchatting themselves using your product or service? That means extending what you are doing to not just cultivating customers but actively cultivating advocates. This is not difficult to do when you have learned the trick. At Bluewolf we've broken it down into three simple steps:

1. Find out how your customers want to be engaged.
   When someone becomes a new customer, be sure to thank and welcome them. With all of the marketing noise out there, it's essential to show your appreciation for their business. But don't stop there. Develop a cadence of personalized messaging based on their experience with your brand. Consider even asking customers how they want to engage with you. This can be achieved through a

subscription-management strategy. Discover what they want to gain from being your customer.

2. Develop personalized engagement plans.
As your relationships with your customers grow, track their activity patterns. Monitor how they choose to interact with your brand by taking into account both their demographic and engagement data. Not all customers should be treated the same or want to be treated the same. Identify different customer types and develop a personalized engagement plan to increase customer satisfaction. These engagement plans can morph into instances of customer advocacy, but definitely take your cue from the customer.

3. Deliver what your customers want from you.
Discover what they are hoping to gain as customers of your brand, and then identify how you can help them get the most out of their experience. As you get to know your customers in a more personalized and intimate way, make it a goal to proactively engage them. It's not enough just to keep up with customers' demands in today's hyperconnected global marketplace. You have to know what your customers want before they do to ensure long-term engagement. This way, you'll be well equipped to align your brand with your customers' success by demonstrating your investment in their future goals or aspirations.

A few more suggestions for encouraging customer advocacy: Know what they might like to do and tie ideas for advocacy to the customer's measurable business objectives. Help your clients answer the question, "How can I help our brand most?" Notice I wrote *our brand* because they, indeed, have a stake in the success of the brand, too. Of course, start small and then scale up. For most companies, advocacy programs are the focus of a single department—and that's a great start. As programs grow, integrate them into every initiative and campaign, then implement them across the organization so sales, service, and marketing all have a role in building a community of customer advocates.

THE CUSTOMER JOURNEY

As with much of what I preach, let's start with data. As I noted previously, digital is king, and the customer experience is the crown jewel. Marketing leaders today already are embracing these two truths as evidenced in the latest *The State of Salesforce* study. For instance: successful marketers are connecting with customers in new ways across mobile, e-mail, social, and the web. In the study, 73 percent say a customer journey strategy has positively impacted overall customer engagement, making it the second biggest priority for marketers this year.

Although I generally try to downplay technology, sometimes you just can't avoid it. Among *The State of Salesforce* respondents, the top teams are more likely to extensively use marketing analytics and predictive intelligence among other tools as they seek to bridge the gaps between marketing, sales, and service. Of the top performers 64 percent say they are excellent at creating a single view of the customer, versus only 4 percent of underperformers. Along the same lines, leading marketers also understand the value of a cross-channel approach. In fact, top teams are 3.2 times more likely than underperformers to strongly agree they've integrated their social media activity into their overall marketing strategy; 3.4 times more likely to integrate e-mail marketing; and 5 times more likely for mobile marketing. Among high performers who have integrated their digital marketing channels with their overall marketing, at least 95 percent rate the integrations as very effective or effective.

Did you think mobile was a passing fad? Not *The State of Salesforce* leaders. From 2015 to 2016, every aspect of mobile covered in this research rose significantly in usage. This growth encompasses both mobile as a marketing platform (such as mobile apps) and mobile as a marketing channel (such as SMS). This amounts to 98 percent growth in mobile app usage and 111 percent growth in SMS usage; a majority of marketers are now using these mainstream mobile tactics to engage customers. To make a great one-two punch, marketers are combining e-mail personalization capabilities even as they grow more sophisticated and the channel becomes ever more integral for marketers to deliver a holistic customer journey. Top teams are 4.2 times more likely than underperformers to leverage predictive intelligence or data science to create personalized e-mails, while 49 percent of marketers say e-mail is directly linked to their business's primary revenue source—a notable jump from the 20 percent of marketers who said the same in 2015 (Figure 11.1).

In 2015, three of the top five areas where marketers planned to increase their spending involved social outlets. Those investments appear to be paying off; 75 percent of marketing leaders report that social is generating return on investment (ROI). Top teams are also 1.7 times more likely than underperformers to align their social media marketing strategy with other social activities, such as customer service, in pursuit of a more unified customer view. So it should be no surprise that nearly two-thirds

Figure 11.1 *The State of Salesforce* **2015–2016**

of marketers are boosting budgets for advertising on social platforms in 2016, making it the third largest area for increased investment. Among high performers, 80 percent will increase spending on advertising on social platforms. In order to create a unique experience based on real customer identity, 83 percent of top teams use customer data (such as e-mail or phone data) to segment or target ads.

By now you're pretty deep into this book. (Thank you for sticking with me.) How many times have I harped on customer obsession and the customer journey? I hope you're not sick of it yet, because it's important. Let me reiterate that message in yet another way: Customers expect a personalized and consistent experience with brands, across all channels and departments. As enterprises race to deliver those seamless digital customer experiences, they're realizing that technology only takes them part of the way to those customer moments, while every touch point drives deeper engagement and repeat business. In fact, 82 percent of marketers say customer engagement is a key success metric for their role; maybe the only metric ahead of that would be customer satisfaction or repeat business.

So how do you stimulate customer engagement? It starts with something I've said numerous times in this book: Dig into your data; not just superficial data, the easy demographic and company data. No, dig into *all* of the data you have collected from *every* customer touch point to create a meaningful persona profile. If data is still locked in corporate silos, break them down right now, even if you have to tap a C-level champion to get access to it. You need to get not only marketing's data, but data from accounting, sales, tech support, and training—everywhere the organization and customer intersect. And much of this data is unstructured. The end result is more than a single view of the customer—that's only the foundation, and honestly, no one ever looks at the proverbial 360-degree view of a customer anyhow. Rather, the end result is a prescriptive action that guides an end user, and employee, toward what we call "an extraordinary customer moment."

MARKETING CAMPAIGNS (OR, HOW YOU STRUCTURE AND MEASURE YOUR MARKETING INITIATIVES)

Now that I have beaten you up about the customer experience and customer obsession, are you ready to adjust your marketing campaigns? In the recent past, marketers would almost automatically focus their campaign on building brand or product awareness among their target customers. Others might direct their campaigns to generate inquiries or even direct sales. These are perfectly valid marketing goals. A few more leading-edge marketers might aim their campaigns to support their digital brand image online or directly engage their customers and prospects in online interactive activities and gamification. The goal is to begin building the personal relationship from the start in a way that can be directed toward your desired business outcomes.

Another option is to revise your approach to the conventional marketing funnel. Too often, marketing departments are focused on the final stages before closing. We've talked about this earlier, but we can be more specific here. Successful businesses focus on the early stages of the sales cycle. After all, not all prospects are ready for your message when they first encounter it. Some need to let ideas percolate for a while. In the meantime, which may be weeks or even months, you can use digital marketing and social media to engage their interest in various ways with appropriate content. This is called a nurturing strategy. The idea is to focus not only on the opportunities close to conversion but also on the lead time required to turn inquiries into genuine interest. For this you may send selected pieces of content along with ideas that might be of interest periodically over months or even two or three years. The length of the nurture campaign doesn't matter since all you are sending are well-targeted, personalized e-mail messages, not spam. As you learn more about this prospect, you will be able to nudge him or her closer toward becoming an active prospect able to move to a conversion track. This type of demand funnel entails close collaboration between sales and marketing as they work hot and not-so-hot prospects (see Figure 11.2). This is yet another reason to eliminate silos.

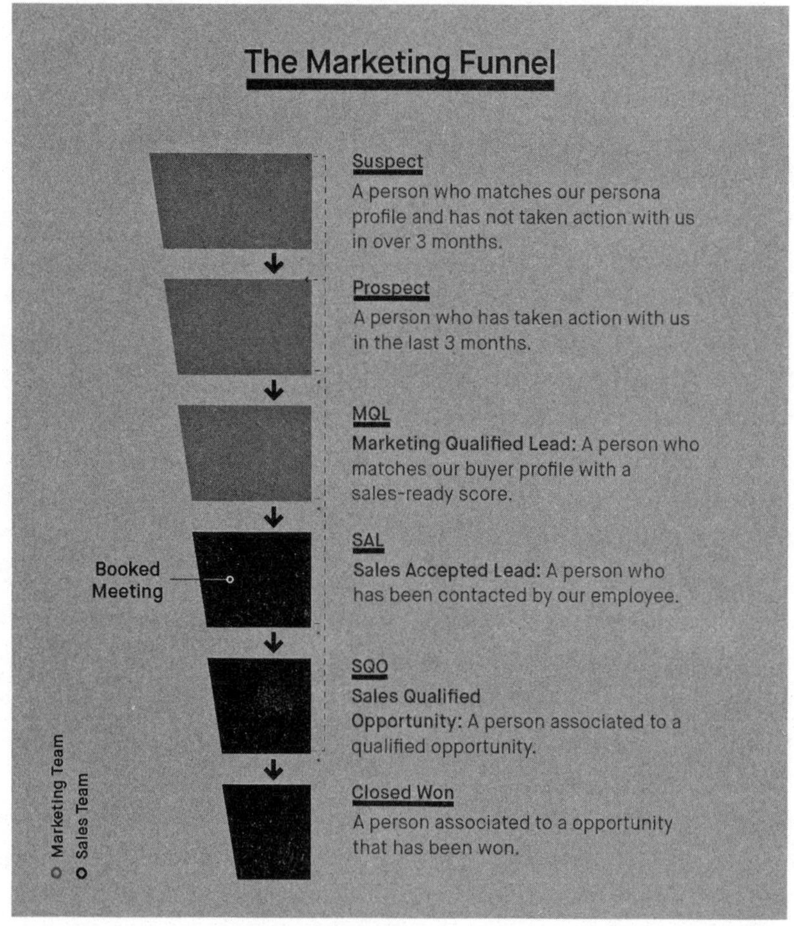

Figure 11.2

As it turns out, we're really talking about a new marketing process. There are so many points of contact between prospects and your marketing efforts that this model, the nurture approach, focuses on the time between the first touch point and genuine interest, which could be a few years. To make this work, constant monitoring of sentiment is essential. This is how you pick up the evolving mind-set of the prospect you are nurturing. Watson, for example, takes a daily dump of all Twitter feeds, which can then be targeted to analyze specific products, features, or interests that can be used to score leads and enrich data for nurturing or outreach.

LEVERAGING TECHNOLOGY

The technology I'm talking about here is data and marketing automation. Current digital marketing methodology, much as it is practiced at Bluewolf, dictates the need for a strategy that does four things: finds the right audience, uses the right channel, delivers the right content, and does all of that at the right time. To determine a strategy for your organization that encompasses all four things, you need data. Data determines the channel, audience, content, and timing. Top-performing marketing organizations recognize that a data strategy is required in order to bring a sophisticated and disruptive digital campaign to life, and to achieve maximum engagement and lift. If that's not enough, here are four reasons you want to do this:

1. Mitigate risk by understanding what's working and what isn't by testing campaigns and monitoring performance prior to scaling. This will allow you to achieve your goals through a phased approach and exploit tactics that have proven to work.
2. Increase one-to-one personalized content that connects with target personas by leveraging customer data.

3. Gain an exhaustively thorough view of the customer by monitoring campaign performance and capturing customer data in a centralized system of record.
4. Understand the consumer on a deeper level in order to anticipate their needs in the future and improve brand loyalty.

As much as I have tried to downplay the role of technology, it's absolutely necessary for marketing automation and cannot be ignored. So, start by partnering with IT. Digital marketing teams cannot be effective without the support of their peers in IT. Collaboration and partnership are key to successful campaign execution and data governance.

Also, think of marketing as a science, not an art, and apply the scientific method by determining a hypothesis, testing it, and validating it through performance monitoring before making significant investments and scaling your strategy. This approach results in a higher probability of campaign ROI and helps you avoid costly mistakes. Finally, build a system-of-record. Be sure to build it for your consumers in your customer relationship management (CRM) platform and integrate it into your marketing technology. This is the best way to gain a complete profile of your consumers and to more effectively market to them in the future.

Marketing automation is not just a source of leads, although leads can result from it. It's a platform/set of tools used to nurture prospects with highly personalized, useful content that helps convert prospects to customers and turn customers into delighted ones. The data is the raw material that enables you to design and automate effective, personalized e-mails, social content, ads, everything else that brings the customer closer to you. You can also use the social sentiment data captured from LinkedIn, Twitter, Facebook, and the others to send targeted ads directly to your customers on their preferred social media platforms. The same applies to e-mail marketing by creating customized e-mail message content based on your customer data. Williams-Sonoma, for example, uses e-mail templates to populate messages based on a customer's interests and purchasing and browsing history. In this way, your automation can directly feed your funnel. For example, create a set of messages to respond to those common situations that frustrate the conversion process, like items left in a shopping cart or requested information that hasn't been clicked on. The personalized message can prod the customer along toward the next step and get these fence sitters off the damn fence.

One of Bluewolf's clients, a global leader and the inventor of fiber cement siding and backerboard, offers a good example. The company's products are used in a number of markets, including new residential construction, repair, and remodel, and a variety of commercial applications, but it doesn't actually sell them to homeowners. It sells through a network of partners, homebuilders, and contractors. As a result, the company is not in the room with its buyer, and it noticed that its voice and value proposition were getting diluted throughout the sales process.

Given the intense emotional experience of home remodeling, this company felt it was crucial for it to connect with homeowners on a deeper level. In order to increase market share, the company needed a digital strategy to engage homeowners while simultaneously supporting clients and partners at each stage of the buying cycle: from inspiration through evaluation, decision making, and postpurchase. Although the business already had Salesforce and Marketo, there was inconsistent integration between the systems, and the communication strategy was uneven.

(*continued*)

(continued)

The company envisioned a way to differentiate its brand among its peers and maintain its leadership in the industry. They wanted to generate loyalty and advocacy, but they also knew they needed to leverage Salesforce and Marketo in a more integrated way in order to be successful—that's when they called Bluewolf.

Our team helped this company develop a digital marketing plan that identified three areas of focus: lead acquisition, nurture, and partner advocacy. The initial phase included a lead generation campaign called the Ambassador Program, where designated brand ambassadors would go door to door with an iPad app allowing people to register if they wanted more information about siding. Once a new lead came into Salesforce and Marketo from the app, information was automatically sent to the lead via Marketo, and then the lead was moved into the nurture program. The second phase included the launch of a new website that targeted the consumer (business-to-consumer) or homebuyer. The site was redesigned to showcase new creative content, from brochures to color samples, and engage the visitors in the home remodeling excitement and experience, like picking colors, and encourage them to provide basic contact information for follow-up.

With an average buying cycle of 12–36 months, it also was important to maintain the conversation with the lead without overwhelming them. Using Marketo's e-mail and lead management capabilities, we created a multitouch drip campaign that tapered off if the lead became disengaged. On the other hand, if the lead chose to pursue a project with one of its partner contractors, updates and tips were sent to the lead with each new stage they completed in Salesforce. This trigger-based campaign was key in keeping the lead informed and excited about the life-changing journey they were about to undertake. At the same time, Bluewolf also worked with the company to strengthen its partner advocacy program in key markets through a pilot campaign that incentivized builders to use 100 percent company-produced products. If builders used both siding and trim products, the company would insure that sale with a 10-year service commitment, which was in addition to the standard warranty. This gave partners both confidence and peace of mind, improving the company's positioning among partners and homeowners, and helping it to establish a trustworthy relationship.

This building products company provides a good object lesson, but there are many more. Here are three that recognized the value of personalized communication at the right time and in the right place and are using a suite of Salesforce tools to better connect with customers and prospects:

In an effort to increase sales, McDonald's is shifting its customer engagement strategy from large-scale mass media to personalized communication via mobile, e-mail, and social. This alone may not strike you as innovative—who doesn't use those three channels for sales and customer outreach? However, by using Social.com and Active Audiences, McDonald's is leveraging its CRM data to coordinate personalized messaging across all devices and platforms.

If you're within range of a McDonald's restaurant, your location will trigger a push notification to your phone, and ads will stream into your Facebook and Instagram feeds. Rather than having to wait until you pass a billboard on the highway or a poster in the subway to catch your attention, McDonald's is reaching out to customers in the moment. Not only does this help increase store traffic, but it's also a lot more relevant to individuals who can now walk into a store a block away and satisfy a craving, instead of salivating on a train platform.

Mattel, meanwhile, focuses on creating and nurturing lifelong customer journeys. From Fisher-Price to adult collectibles, the company wants customer relationships that last for life. Using Salesforce Journey Builder, Mattel is engineering a customer journey that begins the moment you place an order. The confirmation e-mail includes a banner asking you to download Mattel's mobile app. Further communications are sent using date-based triggers (ship date, delivery date, etc.) to encourage further interaction via mobile and social.

Here's how it works: Once you receive your order—say, a Hot Wheels car—you can scan the QR code in the app and race the car you just bought on a digital track. They've leaped beyond the competition by incorporating their physical toys into a digital experience. They have created a unique sense of personal ownership that spans a customer's physical and digital realities, providing a seamless experience that promotes and inspires deeper engagement.

Finally, using Social Studio, Alex and Ani, a boutique jewelry company, responds to every customer who interacts with them online. They know that the most powerful voice is the customer voice and prioritize customer comments, concerns, and ideas accordingly. They have always understood the power of customer advocacy and are using Social Studio to boost its influence.

For instance, Social Studio allows Alex and Ani to track, analyze, and engage with every single social media post from its customers and prospects. Did you tweet about an issue? Not only will the company send your comment to its customer care team, but it will halt all other promotional outreach until your problem is resolved. Did you post a killer photo wearing one of its pieces? The company will give you a shout out and also ask if it can use your image on its website. Alex and Ani defines itself as "an emotion and meaning based company, delivering that through jewelry." Now it's using Social Studio to deliver more on that promise.

Is there a lesson here? You bet. Regardless of its industry or approach, each of these companies is prioritizing individual connections to improve and sustain customer relationships. Deep, personalized engagement is not only possible even in this age of mass everything, it's now a requirement for long-term success.

MULTICHANNEL, OMNICHANNEL, UNIVERSAL

Some people, usually those associated with technology vendors, insist there is a significant difference between multichannel, omnichannel, and universal marketing, but they all seem to try to reach customers and prospects through multiple channels. Multichannel came first, but it has been superseded in recent years by omnichannel. Universal is coming on strong as the newest contender. All of these terms imply the use of multiple communication channels to reach your audience based on the idea that audience members use different channels throughout the day, and your messages and their timing should be targeted to the right channel at the right time for the particular message.

This isn't anything radically new. Marketers were targeting audiences with different messages in different media long before the rise of digital. A more worthwhile discussion might be had around the idea of a mobile-first strategy based on research that suggests how deeply mobile has penetrated into customer behavior.

For me, it has become a no-brainer that mobile is one of the top disruptors currently affecting enterprise customer–business interaction. Mobile devices and apps are getting smarter, and capabilities like GPS, combined with customer data and analytics, are adding context and intelligence to mobile experiences. Cloud, social, and mobile are immediately available at customers' fingertips, and the result is higher expectations and less patience with unsatisfactory service.

More than just an emerging channel, mobile is believed by 71 percent of salespeople to be crucial to accessing real-time data about their customers on their mobile devices (Figure 11.3). While such mobile-first thinking is top of mind for enterprises, it often ends up being lower on the priority list because many companies lack a collaborative, organization-wide approach and a robust mobile strategy that could truly capitalize on mobile opportunities.

Every effective mobile strategy starts with identifying moments that support business-level goals and can be tied to business impact. While it's easy to head straight down the architecture or device path, evaluating business processes and interactions between employees, partners, and customers is critical to achieving impactful mobile initiatives. In short, it's not just about the mobile devices. It's about putting yourself in your customers' and employees' shoes as one of the most impactful ways to identify the moments of value along with the barriers to and areas for immediate and measurable gains within business processes. This is essential to turning broken interactions into frictionless, extraordinary moments.

Spoiler alert: I'm going to harp on data again. Great mobile initiatives are only as good as the data behind them. Data is a

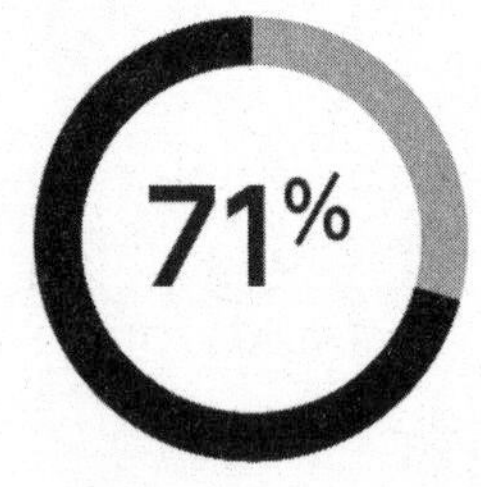

of salespeople believe mobile is crucial to accessing real-time data about customers

Figure 11.3 ***The State of Salesforce*** **2015–2016**

shared responsibility across all departments, and providing all employees, partners, and customers with accurate and relevant data that enables their goals should be the backbone of a company's mobile strategy. Still, while accurate data is important, don't put your vision on hold. Rather, use it as a means to justify a data project and then adopt an ongoing iterative process to rolling out mobile. By achieving a single and accurate view of customers, coupled with the ability to deliver relevant and actionable data from many systems to employees via mobile, you can dramatically differentiate your business and the resulting customer experience provided.

In a 2015 survey by *The Economist*, 54 percent of global executives interviewed confirmed their view that mobile apps are essential. However, only 26 percent actually have apps deployed. This results in an app gap that suggests delivering mobile initiatives, or at least the apps that drive those initiatives, is not so easy. To counter this app gap, companies need to establish organization-wide guidelines around the primary components of mobile IT strategy (devices, apps, data, resources). These guidelines for mobile delivery will then serve as the decision-making framework for every mobile initiative. The result will produce a consistent implementation methodology that can deliver engaging mobile experiences and increase the quality of apps across an organization.

Remember how I started the previous chapter talking about design? Here's why. Poor design choices are never more swiftly punished than in the mobile context. Mobile users tend to be time poor and task oriented, and great mobile design makes information clearer to understand, data easier to consume, and adoption simple. None of these can be achieved without doing the heavy-lifting data analysis up front. That's why a smart user experience is as much about data as it is about design. The focus of the UI/UX design team working on mobile apps should be to gather analytics and user research to better determine design focus and usability decisions.

It also doesn't end with the app deployment. A mobile application launch is just the beginning of a company's mobile journey. User acceptance and relevant metrics are the key to ensuring that all mobile initiatives bring value to customers and the business. Quantitative metrics (sales figures, productivity numbers, etc.) and qualitative results (customer and employee reviews) will continually need to be tracked to focus further releases, plan future apps, and identify the ROI.

Assume future apps are a given. User expectations are always changing. This constant change combined with new mobile technology and increasing market pressures means businesses need a strategic plan for managing existing apps and bringing continued innovation to mobile experiences. This includes frequent updates and new functionality of the mobile tools used to engage customers, as well as regular feedback from stakeholders, partners, and customers to ensure mobile apps stay ahead of customers' and employees' needs. Meanwhile, your competitors will be quite aware of whatever you're doing and will be trying to out-innovate you if they can. To ensure you stay ahead of the curve, mobile-engagement initiatives require the involvement of the entire organization. Both cloud and mobile technologies require a new business-consulting approach to innovate business processes, get an edge on the competition, and exceed bottom-line results.

CONTENT MARKETING

Every effective digital strategy is driven by content marketing. Content is what keeps your visitors coming to your website and, hopefully, returning often and telling their friends to come, too. Good content shapes what they think about your business, your product, your brand, and your position as a brand leader. Just a few pieces of content, no matter how good, won't do the trick. Every time visitors comes to your website, they want to find something new, interesting, and exciting. It is what brings them there and gets them to tell others to do likewise. To that end, you need massive volumes of content that *must* deliver value.

This might seem intimidating and discouraging. I have an associate who put two children through college just by creating fresh content for a variety of businesses. His pitch was that you always need fresh content. Sorry, that's not true. There is a trick to developing good content. The key is not to focus on producing more content, but to maximize the impact of your existing content by using these three Rs of content marketing: repurpose, reuse, and rewrite (Figure 11.4).

With the excessive amount of noise out there, you need to creatively repurpose and reuse your content to optimize its reach. For instance, a webcast can live long past its short shelf life if you gate the recording, turn it into a blog series to recap the content, expand it into a white paper around the key findings from the expert speakers, or even leverage the content in an ongoing e-mail campaign to those who did not attend. Be imaginative and repurpose your content into a series of podcasts or Pinterest walls. The point is to repackage it to extend the life and the reach of its message.

Complementary to curating your content, you must also take advantage of the breadth of available channels to drive ongoing demand generation. Bluewolf CMO, Corinne Sklar, frequently speaks on the topic: "I always tell my marketing team that they

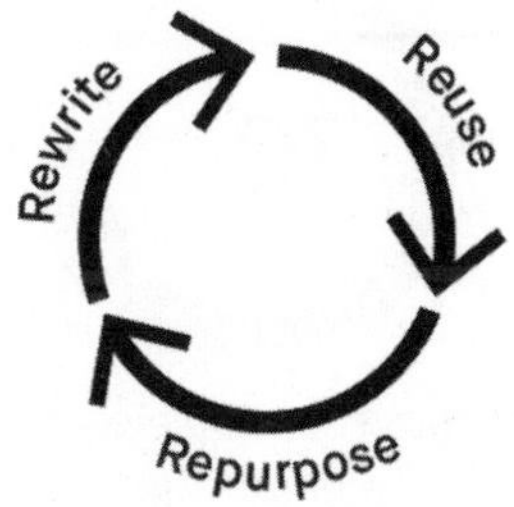

Figure 11.4 The 3 Rs of Content Marketing

must 'pluck the chicken off the bone' before moving on to developing a new content piece."[1] Don't spend valuable resources on new content creation without making absolutely sure you're getting the most possible value out of each piece you already have. Consider your newest piece of content and ask yourself, "How much value have I gotten out of it, and how can I identify four more ways to spin it into something new?"

Keep in mind that at the end of the day, you are still communicating with fellow human beings, so connect with them, both personally and through their unique business needs. Your content strategy and nurture paths are meant to build trust and loyalty between your potential customers and your brand, so make sure you drive a personalized conversation through relevant and emotionally engaging content.

Bluewolf's *Essential Guide to Customer Obsession* found that behavioral economists believe that up to 70 percent of customer decisions are based on emotional factors (Figure 11.5). With that in mind, building trust between your brand and your audience suddenly becomes paramount. So skip those robotic-sounding e-mails and leverage an emotional connect through appropriate content to drive loyalty, increase engagement, and elevate your brand exposure.

Building a strong connection and loyalty to your brand will also result in higher rates of consideration, purchase, and

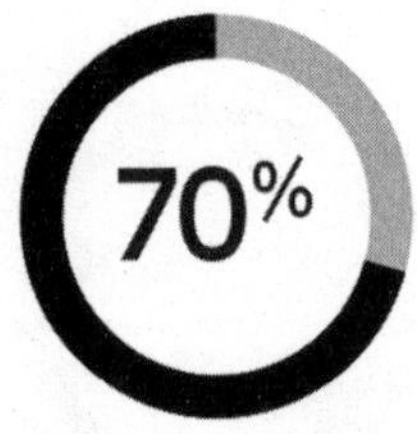

Figure 11.5 *The State of Salesforce* **2015–2016**

willingness to pay a premium. McKinsey found that in 2012, strong brands outperformed weak brands by 20 percent, which is a significant increase from 13 percent in 2011. Furthermore, invest in your brand by cultivating and building a community of brand advocates through trusted quality services and products while continually refreshing their enthusiasm with exciting and compelling content.

Most important, build the personal connection by listening to your audience. Use social data mining as a way to leverage the trends, conversations, sentiments, and issues surrounding your brand. Pay particular attention to the terminology favored by your audience and use it to communicate based on their interests. For example, if you're in the soft drink business, knowing which parts of your audience in which markets around the world refer to soft drinks as "soda" or "pop" can make a big difference in the effectiveness of your content. Edwin Chen, formerly a data scientist for Twitter and Google, created a map of soft drink terms used across the world to illustrate how powerful and useful social data mining tools can be when analyzing human interactions and behavior (Figure 11.6).[2]

Using data like Chen's could help soft drink companies create targeted, regional campaigns that reflect local speech patterns. Once you gain insight into whether your intended audience drinks "soda" or "pop," you can begin a fluid (no pun intended) conversation with them that feels natural and colloquial.

As you revisit your content strategy and nurture programs, make sure that your nurture paths are not only customized by buyer type, but that your content, messaging, and calls to action are all fully customized. Leverage the moments you have in front of your customer, and continue to build your digital relationship with them. Don't be afraid to reshare a piece of content with them. Most likely, they will appreciate the reminder to read a high-quality piece of content that is directly relevant and personalized to their needs and interests.

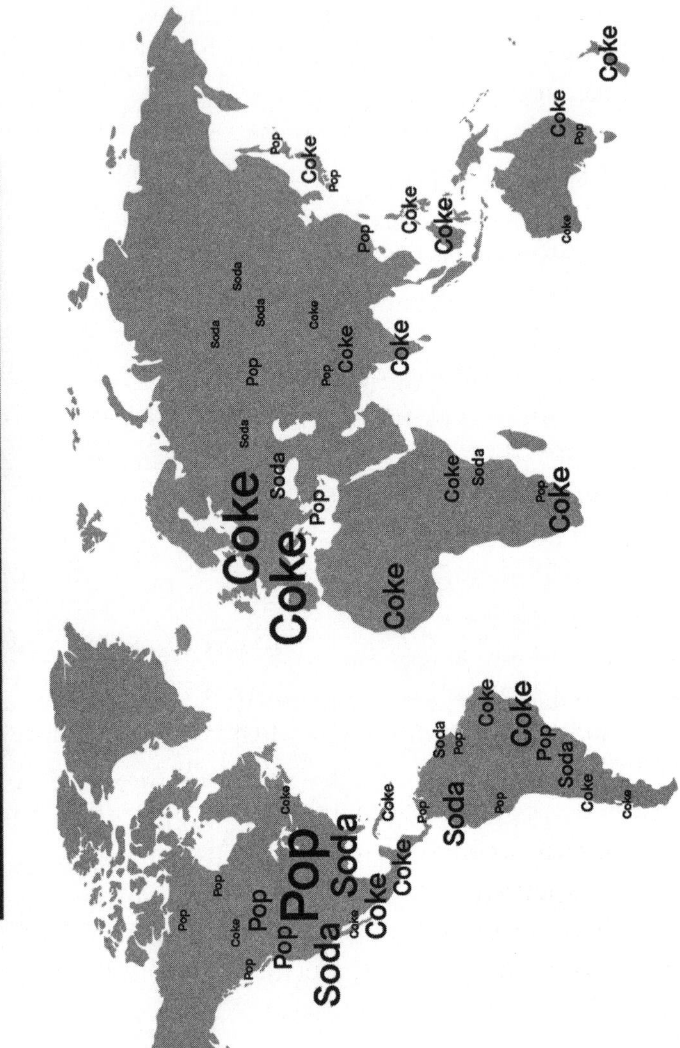

Figure 11.6 Global Soda Terminology Map, Edwin Chen, 2015

To make any of this work, you will have to answer a few questions: Who are these visitors? Why should they care? What's the best way to target/reach them? And what's their preferred vernacular around this topic? Want a hint about the answer? These visitors may be your customers, but not necessarily; your customers should have other parts of your website that specifically target them. The others might be prospects or not. Maybe they are potential prospects at the earliest stages of nurturing.

This is not a tool and technology issue. Sure, analytics tools can help parse customer conversations, but you need your entire team on board to implement your content strategy. Your team will include the content strategist, copywriter, graphic designers, social media manager, and anyone else who interacts with customers. Make sure to empower your people now, if you have not already done so, to own these customer touch points and the customer moments that result.

Speaking to *CMO* during a 2015 visit to Sydney, Corinne Sklar, our CMO, said: "Too many marketers still perceive technology as a panacea and fail to take into account the wider cultural and operational changes needed to operate successfully in a digital-first environment. . . . The big question is: Do you have the right cadence of execution around doing digital marketing? Do you have a content producer? A copywriter? Or if you're not going to do that internally, who are the partners you're going to work with on that? And do they have that technology expertise in-house?"[3]

Often when she asks these questions, the audience looks at the floor or looks at the ceiling, squirming uncomfortably in their seats. They're uncomfortable because they don't have the answers. That's okay. There is a lot of maturity still evolving around this. The audience should take it as a signal that they have some fast learning to do, and then get started. And while you're at it, *don't forget to take into account the wider cultural and operational changes needed to operate successfully in a digital-first environment.*

Final Thoughts

When a book like this ends, it usually concludes with a few sweeping statements about the future of business and technology. The problem is, most predictions about the future never come true, leaving those books feeling dated and out of touch.

The more pressing question is, what can you do for your business right now to move it forward? How do you keep your finger on the pulse of innovation? In the existing era we're in right now, as world-shaking organizations such as Amazon and Google have expanded over the past 15 years, it's tempting to try to predict the future. And we all have friends who are building cool apps ("Hey check this out, I can order my food from underwater!"), but if we give in to the temptation to live our lives through the crystal ball, we'll end up eating a lot of glass.

Innovation doesn't require predicting the future. Let me take you back a few years. In 2007, my cofounder Michael Kirven and I were featured on the cover of *VAR Business* magazine. Little did we know, the world as we knew it was going to collapse 12 months later. This was a year before the financial crisis, before the market corrected, and before unemployment went to 10 percent—we all know that story. When I think back to what made Bluewolf successful as a consulting firm, it was precisely because we weren't trying to predict the future. We were using tools that were available to us at that point in time.

We were the first company to embrace the cloud back before it was called the cloud, and more than a few people questioned our judgment. "You're a consulting company and you're dealing with SaaS? There's nothing to do! No hardware, software, or storage. What are you going to do?" But we figured out that the cloud was incredible for taking small incremental steps in organizations and driving toward innovation. Having a perfectly networked application like Salesforce that was browser based with a tab interface, point-and-click configuration, and open APIs—in 2007 that was what the world gave us to use in front of customers. That was what we innovated with.

If you had asked me 10 or 15 years ago what the future would hold and I told you that Dell would be a private company with negative growth and that Apple would be the most valuable company on the planet, you would have laughed me out of the room. Falling into the trap of predicting the future is not the same thing as innovating. When we think about innovation at Bluewolf, we start with the customer. How do you start with the customer? Simple. Every single chief executive on the planet is concerned with these four things: acquiring new customers, increasing wallet share among their existing customer base, retaining customers, and reducing costs and creating more efficiencies for how they go to market. The organizations that are growing and driving innovation in their business are focused on business outcomes.

The people who love to predict the future are the pundits, paid to make waves through conversation. If you're a chief executive or entrepreneur, you need to keep yourself abreast of the latest tech developments but can't afford to be distracted by the "maybes." You have to plan for right now, and you have to avoid falling in love with technology for technology's sake. Use your resources to become a problem finder first and a problem solver second. You can't have "vision" without an understanding of how a new technology or process is going to affect people right now, because that's all you really have to go off of. After all, it's not really innovation when you create a solution in search of a problem.

In today's world, decisions happen at the speed that data can be collected and analyzed. Our global business cadence is harnessed to it. And organizations that are rife with hierarchy and antiquated technology and process suffer precisely because decisions take forever. As a leader, take it upon yourself to create what I call *flattened transparency* with your technology. Every critical metric in your business should be accessible through a simple dashboard, from your phone, from anywhere in the world. You should be able to reach into the cloud and see pertinent details about each customer. You should be aware of their sentiment, know how they found your brand, and what they need to stay engaged. The same goes for your employees. Building this flattened transparency will help to legitimize your decision making and make you more relevant and in touch as a leader. It will enable you to engage on the customer battlefield, and you will garner tremendous hands-on respect from your team.

Begin by building a model and putting an analytics engine behind it that can tell you when you have situations or opportunities with your customers. Take all of those data points and touch points, and arrive at a model that is going to tell you what is actually going on with your customers. Then use design in your applications to work with your employees and end users. Reduce the data down to specific customer moments; design systems to take advantage of those moments; and enable your employee, partner, and customer cultures to engage with you through each of them. Design your touch points beautifully and simply, so that the greatest assets in your organization—people and knowledge—can coalesce to provide a constant stream of extraordinary customer moments.

That's how you innovate and reach a future state of success while the rest of the world is still trying to figure out what it's going to look like.

Notes

PREFACE

1. John F. Gantz, Darren Bibby, Chris Ingle, Philip Carnelley, Maria Gabriella Cattaneo, and Bo Lykkegaard, "The Salesforce Economy: How Salesforce, Its Ecosystem of Partners, and Its Customers Will Create More Than 1 Million Jobs and Add $272 Billion to Local Economies in the Next Four Years," IDC White Paper, August 2015, http://www.sfdcstatic.com/assets/pdf/misc/The-Salesforce-Economy-White-Paper.pdf, November 2, 2015.
2. Gantz, et al., "The Salesforce Economy."

INTRODUCTION

1. Mat Honan, "Remembering the Apple Newton's Prophetic Failure and Lasting Impact," *Wired,* August 5, 2013, http://www.wired.com/2013/08/remembering-the-apple-newtons-prophetic-failure-and-lasting-ideals, October 17, 2015.

CHAPTER 1. DISRUPTION AND BUSINESS SUCCESS

1. Jim Clifton, *The Coming Jobs War* (New York, NY: The Gallup Press, 2011), 10–11.
2. Clifton, *The Coming Jobs War*, 10–11.

CHAPTER 2. PEOPLE DRIVE CHANGE, TECHNOLOGY ENABLES

1. "Change.org," *Wikipedia,* https://en.wikipedia.org/wiki/Change.org, June 6, 2016.
2. Zac Hall, "iOS 8 adoption bumps up to 81% with help of Apple Watch," 9TO5Mac, April 29, 2015, http://9to5mac.com/2015/04/29/ios-8-adoption-rate-2, October 10, 2015.
3. Nir Eyal, *Hooked: How to Build Habit-Forming* Products (New York, NY: Penguin Publishing Group, 2014).
4. Eyal, *Hooked.*
5. Adam Bryant, "Joel Peterson of JetBlue on Listening Without an Agenda," *The New York Times,* May 9, 2015, http://www.nytimes.com/2015/05/10/business/joel-peterson-of-jetblue-on-listening-without-an-agenda.html?_r=2, October 24, 2016. *NY Times* JetBlue Chairman interview permission.

CHAPTER 3. WHY SOCIAL MATTERS TO EVERY BUSINESS

1. "Smartphones at the dinner table? Smartphone trendspotting down under," Google Australia blog, September 8, 2011, http://google-au.blogspot.com/2011/09/smartphones-at-dinner-table-smartphone.html, November 19, 2015.
2. Nic Fildes, "Vodafone calls on social media to drive brand further," *The Australian Business Review*, December 11, 2013 http://www.theaustralian.com.au/business/companies/vodafone-calls-on-social-media-to-drive-brand-further/story-fn91v9q3–1226780139454,October 28, 2015.
3. "Number of social network users worldwide from 2010 to 2019 (in billions)," *Statista,* http://www.statista.com/statistics/278414/number-of-worldwide-social-network-users, October 3, 2015.
4. Monica Anderson and Andrea Caumont, "How Social Media Is Reshaping News," Pew Research Center FactTank, September 24, 2014, http://www.pewresearch.org/fact-tank/2014/09/24/how-social-media-is-reshaping-news, October 15, 2016.

5. Thomas Friedman, "Social Media: Destroyer or Creator?" *The New York Times*, February 3, 2016, http://www.nytimes.com/2016/02/03/opinion/social-media-destroyer-or-creator.html, February 5, 2016. Used with permission.
6. Tim Pickard, "10 Customer Service Stats and What They Mean for Your Contact Center," Salesforce blog, January 14, 2015, https://www.salesforce.com/blog/2015/01/ten-customer-service-stats-what-they-mean-your-contact-center-gp.html, October 22, 2015.
7. Eric Berridge, "Going Social: IT's Gauntlet in the Global Era," Computerworld, June 26, 2012, http://www.computerworld.com/article/2471944/social-business/going-social-it-s-gauntlet-in-the-global-era.html, January 7, 2016.
8. Eric Berridge, "Going Social Part II: Fight for the Users," Computerworld, August 16, 2012, http://www.computerworld.com/article/2472467/social-business/going-social-part-ii-fight-for-the-users.html, January 7, 2016.

CHAPTER 4. RETHINKING EMPLOYEE ENGAGEMENT

1. Jim Clifton, *The Coming Jobs War* (New York, NY: The Gallup Press, 2011), 99.
2. Clifton, *The Coming Jobs War*, 100.
3. Clifton, *The Coming Jobs War*, 102.
4. Clifton, *The Coming Jobs War*, 103.
5. Clifton, *The Coming Jobs War*, 105.
6. Stan Slap, *Under the Hood: Fire Up and Fine-Tune Your Employee Culture*, (New York: Penguin Group, 2015): 11. Used with permission.
7. Slap, *Under the Hood,* 12.
8. Slap, *Under the Hood,* 14–15.
9. Slap, *Under the Hood,* 97.
10. Clifton, *The Coming Jobs War*, 102.
11. "Number of Netflix streaming subscribers worldwide from 3rd quarter 2011 to 1st quarter 2016 (in millions), Statista, http://

www.statista.com/statistics/250934/quarterly-number-of-netflix-streaming-subscribers-worldwide, January 21, 2016.
12. Margaret Heffernan, "Why It's Time to Forget the Pecking Order at Work," TED Talk, June 16, 2016, https://www.youtube.com/watch?v=Vyn_xLrtZaY.
13. Vanessa Thompson, "The Opportunities and Challenges of Delivering Superior Experiences: IDC's 2015 EXPERIENCES Survey," IDC Research, Inc., June 2015, http://www.idc.com/getdoc.jsp?containerId=256564, January 22, 2016.

CHAPTER 5. CUSTOMER ENGAGEMENT DEFINED

1. Jennifer S. Lerner, Ye Li, Piercarlo Valdesolo, and Karim Kassam, "Emotion and Decision Making" (draft paper, Harvard University, June 16, 2014), http://scholar.harvard.edu/files/jenniferlerner/files/annual_review_manuscript_june_16_final.final_.pdf, January 20, 2016.
2. Jennifer S. Lerner, Ye Li, Piercarlo Valdesolo, and Karim S. Kassam, "Emotion and Decision Making: Online Supplement," *Annual Review of Psychology* 66 (January 2015): 799–823, http://scholar.harvard.edu/files/jenniferlerner/files/annual_review_supplemental_materials_formatted_oct_24.pdf?m=1420822531, January 25, 2016.
3. Peter Noel Murray, "How Emotions Influence What We Buy," *Psychology Today*, February 26, 2013, https://www.psychologytoday.com/blog/inside-the-consumer-mind/201302/how-emotions-influence-what-we-buy, February 6, 2016.
4. Michelle Parker, "Berkshire Hathaway Travel Protection: Ahead of the Digital Insurance Curve," Bluewolf, September 11, 2015, http://www.bluewolf.com/bluewolf-now/berkshire-hathaway-travel-protection-ahead-digital-insurance-curve.
5. Vera Loftis, "Empowering your Marketing Team to Optimise Customer Experience," *Digital Marketing* Magazine, December 23, 2015, http://digitalmarketingmagazine.co.uk/customer-experience/empowering-your-marketing-team-to-optimise-customer-experience/3028, February 5, 2016.

CHAPTER 6. HOW TO WIN THE TALENT WAR

1. Annie McKee, "How to Hire for Emotional Intelligence," *Harvard Business Review,* February 5, 2016, https://hbr.org/2016/02/how-to-hire-for-emotional-intelligence, February 12, 2016.
2. U.S. Chamber of Commerce Foundation, *The Millennial Generation Research Review,* http://www.uschamberfoundation.org/millennial-generation-research-review, February 12, 2016.
3. Tracy Benson, "Motivating Millennials Takes More than Flexible Work Policies," *Harvard Business Review,* February 11, 2016, https://hbr.org/2016/02/motivating-millennials-takes-more-than-flexible-work-policies, February 18, 2016.
4. Lauren Weber, "What Do Workers Want from the Boss?" *The Wall Street Journal At Work* blog, April 2, 2015, http://blogs.wsj.com/atwork/2015/04/02/what-do-workers-want-from-the-boss, February 21, 2016.
5. Clifton, *The Coming Jobs War,* 186.

CHAPTER 7. GENDER DIVERSITY ISN'T A PLUS, IT'S A BUSINESS IMPERATIVE

1. Claus Wedekind, Thomas Seebeck, Florence Bettens, and Alexander J. Paepke, "MHC-Dependent Mate Preferences in Humans," *Proceedings: Biological Sciences* 260:1359 (June 22, 1995), 245–249, http://links.jstor.org/sici?sici=0962–8452%2819950622%29260%3A1359%3C245%3AMMPIH%3E2.0.CO%3B2-Y, February 17, 2016.
2. Walt Hickey, "The Dollar-And-Cents Case Against Hollywood's Exclusion of Women," FiveThirtyEight, April 1, 2014, http://fivethirtyeight.com/features/the-dollar-and-cents-case-against-hollywoods-exclusion-of-women, February 19, 2016.
3. "Bechdel test," *Wikipedia,* https://en.wikipedia.org/wiki/Bechdel_test, February 22, 2016.
4. Judith Warner, "Fact Sheet: The Women's Leadership Gap," Center for American Progress, March 7, 2014, https://www

.americanprogress.org/issues/women/report/2014/03/07/85457/fact-sheet-the-womens-leadership-gap, February 22, 2016.

5. Warner, "The Women's Leadership Gap."
6. Jonathan Woetzel, Anu Madgavkar, Kweilin Ellingrud, Eric Labaye, Sandrine Devillard, Eric Kutcher, James Manyika, Richard Dobbs, and Mekala Krishnan, "How Advancing Women's Equality Can Add $12 Trillion to Global Growth," McKinsey Global Institute report, September 2015, http://www.mckinsey.com/global-themes/employment-and-growth/how-advancing-womens-equality-can-add-12-trillion-to-global-growth, February 23, 2016.
7. Marcus Noland, Tyler Moran, and Barbara Kotschwar, "Is ener Diversity Profitable? Evidence from a Global Survey," Peterson Institute for International Economics, February, 2016, https://piie.com/publications/wp/wp16–3.pdf, March 1, 2016.
8. "Buying Power: Women in the U.S.," Catalyst.org, May 20, 2015, http://www.catalyst.org/system/files/buying_power_women_0.pdf, March 1, 2016.
9. Anita Williams Woolley, Christopher F. Chabris, Alex Pentland, Nada Hashmi, and Thomas W. Malone, " Evidence for a Collective Intelligence Factor in the Performance of Human Groups," *Science* 330:6004 (October 29, 2010), 686–688, http://science.sciencemag.org/content/330/6004/686.abstract, March 1, 2016.
10. Emily Smykal, "Gender Biases In Recruiting: The Case for Considering More Women," Jibe website, September 17, 2015, https://www.jibe.com/blog/gender-biases-in-recruiting-the-case-for-considering-more-women, March 1, 2016.
11. Corinne A. Moss-Racusin, John F. Dovidio, Victoria L. Brescoll, Mark J. Graham, and Jo Handelsman, Science Faculty's Subtle Gender Biases Favor Male Students," *Proceedings of the National Academy of Sciences* 109:41 (October 9, 2012): 16474–16479, doi: 10.1073/pnas.1211286109, http://www.pnas.org/content/109/41/16474.long, March 2, 2016.
12. "Unconscious Bias @ Work | Google Ventures," YouTube video, September 25, 2014, https://www.youtube.com/watch?v=nLjFTHTgEVU, March 2, 2016.

CHAPTER 8. RIGHT TIME, RIGHT MOMENT, RIGHT CHANNEL

1. "Social Customer Service Performance Report June 2013: US Top 100 Retailers (Selected from Internet Retailer's Top 500," Hubspot, June 2013, https://cdn2.hubspot.net/hub/154001/file-214612143-pdf/Social_Customer_Service_Performance_Report_June_2013.pdf, March 8, 2015.
2. "The State of Customer Service Experience 2015," The Northridge Group, http://www.northridgegroup.com/The-State-of-Customer-Service-Experience, March 8, 2016.
3. Donna Fluss, "Buzzword Battle: Omnichannel Versus Multichannel," *CRM,* August 2014, http://www.destinationcrm.com/Articles/Columns-Departments/Reality-Check/Buzzword-Battle-Omnichannel-Versus-Multichannel-98169.aspx, March 11, 2016.
4. Janine Carlson, "Bridging the Gap Between Customer Service and Social," Bluewolf blog, February 4, 2016, http://www.bluewolf.com/bluewolf-now/bridging-gap-between-customer-service-and-social, March 11, 2016.
5. Kate Leggett, "Trends 2015: The Future of Customer Service," Forrester Research, December 16, 2014, http://www.nice.com/websites/Perfect_experiences/files/Trends-2015-The-Future-Of-Customer-Service-Forrester.pdf, March 13, 2016.
6. Megan Burns, Michael E. Gazala, Carla O'Connor, Ryan Trafton, and Rachel Birrell, "Understanding the Impact of Emotion on Customer Experience," Forrester Research, July 13, 2015, https://www.forrester.com/Understanding+The+Impact+Of+Emotion+On+Customer+Experience/fulltext/-/E-res122503, April 3, 2016.
7. Greg Sterling, "Report: U.S. Smartphone Penetration Now At 75 Percent," Marketing Land, February 9, 2015, http://marketingland.com/report-us-smartphone-penetration-now-75-percent-117746, April 3, 2016.
8. Bob Furniss, "Community Engagement Creates Happy Customers," DestinationCRM.com, January 11, 2016, http://www.destinationcrm.com/Articles/Web-Exclusives/Viewpoints/Community-Engagement-Creates-Happy-Customers-108460.aspx.

9. Natalie L. Petouhoff, PhD, Sharyn Leaver, and Andrew Magarie, “The Economic Necessity of Customer Service,” Forrester Research, January 21, 2009, http://www.iirusa.com/upload/wysiwyg/New%20Media/The%20Economic%20Necessity%20Of%20Customer%20Service_%20Social%20%20Media%20and%20Chat%20Save%20Costs_Better%20Customer%20Experiences%20Petouhoff%202009.pdf, April 4, 2016.

CHAPTER 9. TURNING DATA INTO ACTION

1. “The Zettabyte Era—Trends and Analysis,” Cisco Systems white paper, June 2, 2016, http://www.cisco.com/c/en/us/solutions/collateral/service-provider/visual-networking-index-vni/VNI_Hyperconnectivity_WP.html, June 4, 2016.
2. “What Is Big Data?” IBM website, February 9, 2016, http://www-01.ibm.com/software/data/bigdata/what-is-big-data.html, May 2, 2016.
3. “Gartner Says Actionable Analytics Will Be Driven by Mobile, Social and Big Data Forces in 2013 and Beyond,” Gartner press release, February 11, 2013, http://www.gartner.com/newsroom/id/2332515, May 5, 2016.
4. Tara House, “Get the Real Story from Your Dashboards,” Bluewolf blog, May 9, 2012, http://www.bluewolf.com/bluewolf-now/get-real-story-your-dashboards, May 5, 2016.
5. Joseph Tsidulko, “Salesforce.com Is Bringing Greater Analytics Functionality to Mobile Devices,” *CRN,* February 19, 2015, http://www.crn.com/news/cloud/300075804/salesforce-com-is-bringing-greater-analytics-functionality-to-mobile-devices.htm, May 6, 2016.

CHAPTER 10. HOW GOOD DESIGN CREATES SEAMLESS EXPERIENCES

1. 1866 Map of Central Park, New York, Wikimedia Commons, Geographicus, public domain, https://commons.wikimedia.org/wiki/File:1866_Map_of_Central_Park,_New_York_City,_New

York-_Geographicus_-_CentralParkGuide-mcny-1869.jpg, May 10, 2016.

2. John Maeda, *The Laws of Simplicity* (Cambridge, MA: The MIT Press, 2006), 1.
3. Maeda, *The Laws of Simplicity*, 89.
4. Mark Wilson, "How to Design Happiness," *Fast Company* Co. Design blog, March 29, 2016, http://www.fastcodesign.com/3058237/innovation-by-design/how-to-design-happiness, May 10, 2016.
5. Wilson, "How to Design Happiness."

CHAPTER 11. DIGITAL MARKETING: STANDING OUT IN A SEA OF SAMENESS

1. Cassie Hrushesky, "Lead Nurturing Tips: Building a Successful Content Strategy," Bluewolf, August 14, 2014, http://www.bluewolf.com/bluewolf-now/lead-nurturing-tips-building-successful-content-strategy, May 18, 2016.
2. Edwin Chin, "Soda vs. Pop with Twitter," Edwin Chen blog, July 6, 2012, http://blog.echen.me/2012/07/06/soda-vs-pop-with-twitter, May 12, 2016.
3. Nadia Cameron, "Bluewolf CMO: Technology and Data Won't Fix a Poor Marketing Strategy," *CMO*, November 9, 2015, http://www.cmo.com.au/article/588484/bluewolf-cmo-technology-data-won-t-fix-poor-marketing-strategy, May 18, 2016.

Acknowledgments

This book is the culmination of so many moments at Bluewolf over the last 15 years. Our story as a company is not terribly unique. We have only followed the path that so many other companies have followed in the pursuit of entrepreneurial ideas mixed with collaboration and the need to "put food on the table."

Along the way we believe that we found better ways of doing things for both ourselves and our customers. Client engagement, customer experience, and employee engagement are the three areas where we have excelled and where we are passionate as consultants.

Halfway through writing this book we achieved an incredible milestone at Bluewolf when we were acquired by the most trusted and storied technology company in the world: IBM. While the details surrounding this event are a story unto itself, it goes without saying that our future as an IBM company is bright. We are proud of this milestone and how it validates our vision, and excited about how we can shape a bigger future in customer experience with IBM iX and Salesforce.

There are too many people to acknowledge as contributors to this text, but I will give it my best shot: My parents, who valued education above all else, which benefits me every day; my wife,

Melissa, and our three children Scottie, Emmeline, and Charlie; my bosses over the years, each of whom were mentors and who left me with advice that I use every day: Stacey Estrella, Noosheen Hashemi, Greg Herrera, Paul Hoffman, David Dewalt, Kevin Kern, Danny Turano, Joe Dibartolomeo, Lindsey Armstrong, Kevin Dwyer, and Scott Matthews. Just about every person I've ever met at Salesforce—and there are hundreds—all of whom have taken the leadership of Marc Benioff and built an everlasting technology company that is so much more important than we realize. And thanks to Marc himself for pushing me out of my comfort zone and teaching me the value of customer and employee success.

There are hundreds of "pack members" at Bluewolf to whom I owe a debt of gratitude. My team: Greg Kaplan, Jolene Chan, Corinne Sklar, Glen Stoffel, Paulo Kaiser, Lou Fox, Caryn Fried, and Vaibhav Nalwaya are incredible people and the most trusting and loyal individuals one could imagine. My cofounder, Michael Kirven, has shared more hours with me than anyone but my family, and I thank him immensely for being the tireless worker and trusted partner for the decade that we shared an office, a company, and a life. There were many more laughs than sorrows, and for that I am blessed.

Last, and most important, with regard to this book, thank you to Erin Pendleton for being the incredible writer, organizer, and thought-provoker that made it happen. You are a joy to work with and this project is a product of your hard work and creative self.

Index

Note: Page references in *italics* refer to figures.

INDEX